Chapters in Fox River Valley History

[Separate No. 152]

Chapters in Fox River Valley History

I. William Powell's Recollections

II. Pioneers and Durham Boats on Fox River, by John Wallace Arndt

[From the Proceedings of the State Historical Society of Wisconsin for 1912, pages 146-220]

Madison
Published for the Society
1913

[Separate No. 152]

Chapters in Fox River Valley History

I. William Powell's Recollections
II. Pioneers and Durham Boats on Fox River, by John Wallace Arndt

[From the Proceedings of the State Historical Society of Wisconsin for 1912, pages 146-220]

Madison
Published for the Society
1913

William Powell's Recollections

In an Interview with Lyman C. Draper[1]

Peter Powell,[2] my father, was born in England in 1778. Coming to what is now Wisconsin in 1800, he engaged in the Indian trade, his earliest post being at White Rapids on Menominee River, about eighty miles from Green Bay; he made his returns at Mackinac and passed his summers at Green Bay settlement. At first he was a clerk for Jacob Franks,[3] but afterwards en-

[1] In the Society's annual report for 1878 (*Wis. Hist. Colls.*, viii, p. 53) is the following: "The secretary, during the past year, * * * made a visit to Capt. Wm. Powell, of Shawano County, a native o Wisconsin, now bordering closely on three score and ten, and intimately connected with the Menomonees and other Wisconsin tribes since 1819, and noted down a lengthy statement of his dictation, embracing his recollections of the Menomonees and their prominent Chiefs, Col. Robert Dickson, the British leader of the Northwestern Indian tribes during the War of 1812-15, and the derivation and meaning of many Indian geographical names in Wisconsin having a Menomonee origin." The interview which Doctor Draper took down in notes at the time, has ever since remained only in manuscript. In editing this document for the present publication, we have combined therewith a letter written by William Powell some years later to the present Editor, detailing some additional facts in the lives of both father and son. In working both sources into a connected narrative, we have made only such changes as involved re-arranging the material and improving the phraseology of necessary points. It is believed that Powell's Recollections, while not as valuable as those of Augustin Grignon, published in *Wis. Hist. Colls.*, iii, will prove an authoritative and substantial contribution to early Wisconsin history.—Ed.

[2] The brief sketch of Peter Powell in *Wis. Hist. Colls.*, xix, p. 358, was written before this manuscript came to light.—Ed.

[3] For a sketch of this trader see *Id*, xviii, p. 463, note 85.—Ed.

William Powell (1810–1885)

Enlarged from photograph in possession of the Society

gaged in trade for himself. My mother was Mary Jeffrey, a native of Green Bay, and half Menominee. Her father was an Englishman, and her mother belonged to the family of chief Oshkosh. My father and mother were married at Mackinac in 1802. They had a family of eight, five sons and three daughters, of which there are only myself and a younger brother now (1877) living. I was the fourth child and was born near Death's Door at the entrance to Green Bay. My father was returning from Mackinac to Green Bay with my mother—he had taken her with him to Mackinac when he went after his goods; she was taken sick en route, and I was born the twenty-fifth of September, 1810.

My father was with Colonel McKay at the capture of Prairie du Chien.[4] In August, 1819 [July, 1818],[5] Col. Robert Dickson,[6] formerly Indian agent for the British in the War of 1812, visited Green Bay, and advised my father to go to Pembina to trade, saying that he was British agent there,[7] and would do what he could to favor his interests.

In company with Dickson we started from Green Bay in a bark canoe, hiring four French *voyageurs* and a hunter to kill game en route, as we could not carry provisions enough to last during the trip. We coasted Lake Michigan to Mackinac and up Sault St. Mary River into Lake Superior, coasted that lake and through the Lake [of the] Woods and Lake Winnipeg, thence up Red River to Pembina settlement, arriving at that

[4] For a history of the expedition see *Id*, xi, pp. 254–270; xiii, pp. 1–14; and *post*. A sketch of McKay is in *Id*, xix, p. 365, note 12.—Ed.

[5] In his interview with Draper, Powell told him that they left for the Red River country in August, 1819. In the letter written later, however, he gave the date as July, 1818. In the light of his further statements and of other corroborating evidence, it seems probable that the latter was the correct date.—Ed.

[6] Dickson's career is sketched in *Id*, xii, pp. 133–153; additional facts are found in *Id*, xix, xx, *passim*.—Ed.

[7] Dickson was, in fact, agent for Lord Selkirk, and aiding him in his plans for settling the Red River country. About this time Dickson was urging all the prominent traders at Green Bay—Porlier, Lawe, and the Grignons—to remove to Red River and take with them the Menominee tribesmen. See documenth in *Id*. xx, *passim*. Apparently Powell was the only one of the old British traders who acceded to Dickson's request.—Ed.

place the last of September. There father engaged in the Indian trade, having purchased his goods from the Hudson's Bay Company; remained there three years; each spring he went to Hudson Bay with his furs and returned in the fall with his goods.

At the expiration of the three years he started back for Green Bay with his family, by a land route to the headwaters of Minnesota River. Late in November of 1821, we arrived at Lake Traverse, at a trading post then kept by Mr. Joseph D'Raville,[8] who was employed by the Hudson's Bay Company, and we passed the winter at that place. A short time after we arrived at Lake Traverse a man came there from Illinois, by the name of Dixson,[9] with a drove of cattle, on his way to Pembina settlement; but as winter commenced setting in he was obliged to remain there. During the winter he lost more than half of his cattle, killed by wolves and Sioux Indians.

In the spring of 1822 my father sold his carts and horses to Mr. D'Raville and bought two dugouts large enough to carry his family and his goods, descended Minnesota River to its mouth,[10] which emptied into the Mississippi about six miles

---

[8] This was Joseph Renville, a Dakota half-breed who was born near St. Paul about 1779. Educated in Canada, he early entered Dickson's employ and was interpreter and guide for Pike in 1805–06 and for Major Long in 1823. He served in the War of 1812–15 as captain in the British Indian department under Dickson, and afterwards received a pension. About 1819 he gave up this pension, became an American citizen, and in 1822 was one of the founders of the Columbia Fur Company. When this corporation was sold (1827) to the American Fur Company, he retired to Lac qui Parle and there died in 1846. A Minnesota county bears his name. See fuller biographical sketch in *Wis. Hist. Colls.*, xx.—Ed.

[9] On a map published in 1838 by Judson, of the territory west of the Mississippi, is traced a route from Des Moines River to Lake Traverse, marked "McKnight and Dixon's route, 1822." This no doubt refers to the cattle train here noted. Alexander Ross, *Red River Settlement* (London, 1856), p. 73, mentions the arrival in 1822 of a herd of 300 cattle that sold for good prices—the first, he says, that came to the colony.—Ed.

[10] In the Society's Wisconsin Mss., 10B28, is a letter from Peter Powell to John Lawe, dated Lake de Traverse, March 14, 1822. After speaking of the state of things in the Red River country, Powell con-

above St. Paul. That summer my father with all his family, except myself, arrived at Green Bay. He left me with Capt. William Alexander of the Fifth Regiment, U. S. A., who was stationed at Fort Snelling.[11] I was to stay with him until my father should send for me, in order to go to the school which was kept in the garrison for the officers' children.

Soon after my father returned to Green Bay he again engaged in the Indian trade. His wintering places were up the Mississippi, also up Minnesota River as far as the Blue Earth, which empties into it thirty to forty miles above St. Paul. In the spring he made his returns with his furs at Mackinac. In 1826 he stopped buying his goods from the American Fur Company and bought them from Daniel Whitney of Green Bay,[12] who was the only man in the Western Department who dared to oppose John Jacob Astor in the Indian trade. In the spring of 1827 my father built a log house on Lake Butte des Morts and left his family at that place while he wintered at his trading post; returning in the spring he passed the summer with his family at Butte des Morts. That place continued to be his home till his death in September, 1837. My mother survived him several years, was remarried, and died at Green Bay in the summer of 1844.

The French and Fox War[13]

From Iometah, Oshkosh, and other aged Menominee, I learned that the Sauk and Foxes once had a town at Red Banks; later they removed to Green Bay and got into trouble with the French

tinues thus: "there is no prospect of doing anything in this Country. I have past a Miserable winter for starvation. I intend to pass the Spring a Hunting then go down to the Entry of St. Peters this Summer. * * * I am now much distressed, my family are Quite naked & on the point of Starving."—Ed.

[11] Alexander was at this time lieutenant in the 5th Infantry. He was from Tennessee, entered the regular army in 1820, was promoted to a captaincy in 1836, and died two years later.—Ed.

[12] For a sketch of this early Green Bay merchant, see *Wis. Hist. Colls.*, xii, p. 274, note 3.—Ed.

[13] See Louise P. Kellogg, "Fox Indian Wars," in Wis. Hist. Soc. *Proceedings*, 1907, pp. 142-188.—Ed.

and were made to retire to Little Butte des Morts—now Neenah. Here they exacted tribute in the following way: some of their leaders would post themselves on either side of the stream with a long pole, held up and leaning over the water, indicating that the trader's boats must heave to, and pay tribute before proceeding farther. Getting tired of these exactions, the French got up an expedition and drove them off from Little Butte des Morts. The Sauk and Foxes then retired to Big Butte des Morts and at that point renewed their exactions in the same way. At this time there was a Menominee who had married a Sauk wife. The French and Menominee at Green Bay prevailed on him to go to the Sauk and report some pitiful story of bad treatment on the part of his people as a reason why he had retired to Big Butte des Morts to make his future home with his wife's people; and to report also that there were some traders' boats soon coming up, upon which they could levy rich tribute.

In time the flotilla appeared in sight, each canoe covered with an oilcloth over a ridge-pole, like a roof. Beneath this were a body of armed French, while a large body of Menominee and Chippewa marched up the river by land. As soon as the fleet hove in sight of the town, the Menominee spy quietly and unnoticed took his departure, and apprised his countrymen whom he soon met, that the boats were nearing the Sauk and Fox village. Thereupon they hastened and crept into the rear of the place. As the boats came up, and the tribute poles were posted, the French made for the town landing, and the people rushed down to see and meet them. Then the boat coverings were suddenly thrown off, and the soldiers fired on the Sauk and Fox assemblage, who as they fled back to their houses to get their weapons, were met by the Menominee and Chippewa in the rear, and soon overpowered. Some fled to Winneconne, about three miles distant, where many were overtaken and killed. There their bones were left to bleach upon the ground, hence the name —Winneconne, "the place of skulls." Thus the Sauk and Foxes were again driven westward, up the Fox and down the Wisconsin. A part of them went up to Puckaway and Buffalo lakes, and settled there; the rest settled at Sauk Prairie on the Wisconsin, where subsequently they were joined by the others.

Powell's Recollections

War of 1812-15

Chicago Massacre, 1812: Souligny related to me that a splendid-looking woman (who proved to have been an officer's wife), refused to surrender after the Indians attacked the retreating garrison. She stood up in a wagon and defended herself with her sword, cut and slashed with it, and perhaps wounded an Indian or two, when the Indians, who would have preserved her life, felt constrained to shoot her. Souligny spoke of her long, handsome, flowing hair. He likewise referred to her heroism in sacrificing her life rather than yield herself up a prisoner to the Indians. Such an act naturally attracted the attention of the warriors.[14]

Indians under Dickson. During 1812–13 Col. Robert Dickson wintered in a nice piece of timber on the west side of Lake Winnebago, between Garlic Island and Neenah—about half way between the Island and Neenah. He reached there late in 1812 with a large supply of British presents for the Indians, which he distributed liberally; and then the Indians retired for their winter's hunt, being admonished to meet him early in the spring to go upon the warpath.[15] They assembled in large numbers and received numerous presents and supplies; but at Mackinac a large portion of them backed out and returned home, so Souligny and others related, conveying the idea that only the boldest and bravest kept on.

At Fort Meigs, Souligny first met Tecumseh, shook hands with him, and represented that he regarded it as an honor to have met and fought by the side of so noted and brave a man. Tecumseh was tall, fully six feet, and well-formed. Arrived at Fort Meigs, they drew a party of Americans into an ambuscade

[14] Probably this was Mrs. Corbin, wife of a sergeant. Mrs. Kinzie in *Waubun* (Caxton ed., 1901), p. 178, refers to her heroism. She also narrates the resistance of a Mrs. Holt, who hacked and cut with her husband's sword; but she was on horseback, not in a wagon; and moreover she was ultimately saved from death.—Ed.

[15] See Dickson papers in *Wis. Hist. Colls.*, xi, pp. 271–315; xix, pp. 344–346. In xi, p. 278, Dickson dates his letter from Garlic Island, which would seem to indicate that he wintered thereon, not on the mainland. Arndt, *post*, also locates Dickson on the island.—Ed.

[Colonel Dudley's party],[16] but after that failed to make any impression on the fort, only now and then picking off some of the sentinels. Finally as a last resort, Tecumseh formed the novel idea of the pretended fight in the woods—as if the Indians were encountering an American reinforcement—expecting the garrison would hasten out to the relief of their supposed friends. But General Harrison was too wary to be caught in any such trap.[17] During the siege two Menominee were captured by some American Shawnee, but managed to escape. Becoming discouraged, the British Indians wanted to go home, when Colonel Dickson and the British leaders, to divert their attention, led them against Sandusky. There the Indians picked off some of the Americans going for water; but after the British repulse, all retired.[18]

There probably were no Menominee at the taking of Detroit, or at the River Raisin. Souligny and others spoke as though their first service was when Dickson embodied them and led them to Fort Meigs and Sandusky.

Mackinac in 1814. There lived for many years a very aged Winnebago chief, called Caramaunee, at a little village composed of only three or four bark lodges belonging to himself and his sons-in-law, located about two miles east of what is since called Waukau. [Captain Powell suggests that this may be a slight change or corruption for Nahkaw].[19] East of Fox River, about two miles above Omro, is Delhi. Some two miles back [south] east of Delhi was Waukau, on the old Fort Winnebago trail from Green Bay to the Fox-Wisconsin portage. About two miles east [south] of Waukau, on the west bank of [the outlet of] Rush or Mud Lake, near the centre of the stream, was Car-

---

[16] The interpolation is probably that of Dr. Draper, explaining Powell's reference to an ambuscade. For a brief account of the siege of Fort Meigs and Dudley's defeat (May 5, 1813) see C. P. Lucas, *The Canadian War of 1812* (Oxford, 1906), pp. 75–77.—Ed.

[17] Reference is here made to the second siege of Fort Meigs in July; see *Ibid*, p. 78.—Ed.

[18] This relates to the siege of Fort Stephenson, Aug. 1 and 2; *Ibid*. pp. 78, 79—Ed.

[19] Nahkaw was the Indian form of Caramaunee's name; see *Wis. Hist. Colls.*, v, p. 181, note.—Ed.

amaunee's village.[20] He was a large, square-shouldered, stout man, not very tall, but with a powerful frame and long face. While his people were generally regarded as unreliable and thievish, Caramaunee bore a most excellent character, was liked by all traders, and was friendly to the whites. When I saw him last, about 1850, he seemed nearly a hundred years of age. He said he was out with Colonel Dickson in the War of 1812, went with the Menominee to Sandusky, and was at Mackinac when Major Holmes[21] was shot by L'Espagnol.

Caramaunee and L'Espagnol both gave me the following account of the battle on Mackinac Island.[22] When the Americans landed, the Indians and most of the garrison went out to waylay them. The Indians hid behind rocks and boulders on either side of the anticipated route, while the English with cannon were in the rear towards the fort to draw the Americans forward into the net or trap. While in waiting, the few whites left in the fort got alarmed, thought the Americans were approaching in their rear, and sent a messenger in great haste to notify those in front; whereupon nearly all the Indians fled to the rear, ex-

[20] Publius V. Lawson, *Winnebago County* (Chicago, 1908), i, p. 308, says that there was a village at the outlet of Rush Lake as late as 1846. According to John T. La Ronde, *Wis. Hist. Colls.*, vii, p. 350, Caramaunee had by 1828 removed to the Baraboo River.—Ed.

[21] Maj. Andrew Hunter Holmes entered the regular army from Mississippi at the outbreak of the war, and was assigned as captain of the 24th Infantry. In March, 1814, he distinguished himself in a skirmish on the River Thames, Ontario, where he defeated a British force superior in numbers to his own. For this success he was promoted to the rank of major, and assigned to a part in the recovery of Mackinac. He was killed Aug. 4, 1814, and after the recovery of his body, buried at Detroit. The fort on the highest point of Mackinac Island was subsequently, in his honor, named Fort Holmes.—Ed.

[22] The expedition to recapture Mackinac was undertaken against the judgment of the American officers of the Western department, but it was ordered from Washington. The fleet was commanded by Commodore Sinclair; the land forces by Col. George Croghan. Landing on the west side of the island, the Americans advanced (Aug. 4, 1814), against the British who had thrown up rude fortifications. The death of Holmes threw the advance into confusion, whereupon retreat to the ships was ordered.—Ed.

pecting to encounter the Americans there; but it proved to be a false alarm.

L'Espagnol and his nephew, the Yellow Dog (Oshawwahnem),[23] remained in their places of secretion. Oshawwahnem said "Uncle, let us go with the others." "No," said L'Espagnol, "I shall remain; if you wish to go, you can; but you ought to show proper respect for your uncle by standing by him." Soon they saw the Americans approaching by the route along which they were originally expected, with the officers and a small bodyguard in front. The dress of one officer was thickly covered with silver lace, upon which the sun shone and reflected brilliantly. Supposing this to be the principal officer, the young nephew asked of his uncle the privilege of shooting him, as it would be the greatest honor. Among the Indians, it was a custom that when an uncle commanded a nephew to perform any service, however dangerous, he was in duty bound to do it with unquestioned promptitude; and in return the nephew had the right to ask any favor of his uncle, which must as readily be complied with. Hence L'Espagnol promptly acceded to Yellow Dog's request. The nephew was to fire when his uncle should set the example by firing at a plainer dressed officer, who was swinging his sword carelessly by the handle. When L'Espagnol fired, Major Holmes—for so he proved to be —with his epaulette on his shoulder, fell forward dead. His sword and cap were pitched somewhat ahead of him, and L'Espagnol had barely time to dash out, seize them, and hasten away in the rear of the rocks, with his nephew following him. The latter's gun had missed fire, so the bespangled captain escaped unhurt.

When Major Holmes fell, his negro servant ran off with his body, hiding it between a couple of boulders and throwing some leaves and stuff over him. Hence, when the Indians subsequently returned to get his scalp and searched carefully, they

[23] Dr. Draper wrote on the Ms., "It must be an error in Grignon's 'Recollections' [*Wis. Hist. Colls.*, iii, p. 280] that Oshawwahnem was a cousin of L'Espagnol." But Indian relationships were not carefully marked in degree—the difference between nephew and cousin might not be regarded as important. For further information concerning this chief, consult *Id*, x, pp. 499, 500.—Ed.

failed to find it. Shortly after, the Americans sent back a flag of truce from their ships lying at anchor, asking permission to take away Major Holmes's body. This was granted and the Indians who went along with the British guard were surprised when the American party, with the "black meat" (as they termed the negro servant) for their guide, went and uncovered the concealed body within a few feet of where they had repeatedly passed in search of it. Thus L'Espagnol lost his much coveted scalp; but the exploit, and the trophies which he gave to Colonel Dickson, gave him a high reputation among his people. I myself saw in 1819 the sword and cap formerly belonging to Major Holmes, then in Dickson's possession.

The Yellow Dog must have died early, for I have no recollection of ever having seen him. L'Espagnol used to live in the Green Bay region, making his winter hunts up the Wisconsin. He was an excellent hunter and trapper, and really a peaceable and good Indian and popular with the traders. L'Espagnol was not less than six feet two inches in height, rawboned, and powerful. He could pack on his back a deer he had killed, a five-year-old buck, weighing over two hundred pounds. Saketoo, the eldest surviving son of L'Espagnol, and a younger brother, are (1877) living near Keshena.

Prairie du Chien Expedition. I have no knowledge of Colonel McKay's history prior or subsequent to the Prairie du Chien expedition. But I knew Duncan Graham, a Scotchman who married a Sioux woman. He was a small-sized man and while on a visit to Green Bay about 1830, got a power of attorney from Peter Powell, John Lawe, and some of the Grignons for British services, and went to Montreal to collect the claims; but he was never heard of afterwards.[24]

My father, who was in McKay's expedition, used to relate that the [American] gunboat was upon the river above the fort. When the British and Indians (Menominee, Winnebago, Sioux, some Chippewa, and perhaps Potawatomi) were lying around

[24] For facts in regard to the life of Duncan Graham, see *Id*, ix, pp. 299, 467. Peter Powell was employed by Graham in the Red River country, 1818–21, so that Captain William must have known him when a boy. The story of his disappearance is untrue; he died in Minnesota about 1845, at the home of his son-in-law, Alexander Faribault.—Ed.

on the flats, beleaguering the post, the gunboat floated down. Seeing the British and Indians apparently so numerous, those on board of the boat regarded the chance of maintaining the fort as hopeless, so concluded that their best course was to save themselves and boat and pass on down the river. As they passed, the [American] garrison hailed them, and even shot off their cannon at the vessel from the bastions, to make them heave to; but they passed on without stopping. Lewis From [Louis Manaigre], one of the crew or men on the gunboat, whom I later knew well, stated to me that the shot from the American cannon penetrated the stern of the vessel.

When the British first arrived and demanded a surrender the American commander refused; thereupon Colonel McKay had a furnace erected to heat balls with which to attempt to fire the fort. Seeing the gunboat had deserted them, the garrison concluded it was best to surrender, and did so just as the British had got ready to fire their hot shot. Peter Powell used to say that had the gunboat taken its place near the fort, it could have done effectual work in beating back the British and Indians, and he thought, would have saved the garrison. I have heard the Menominee speak of Colonel McKay as a brave, good leader and instance the fact that when the Americans fired their cannon, the Indians would dodge behind some protection, or fall upon the ground; but Colonel McKay himself would remain standing, erect and fearless. On the way to Prairie du Chien, there was but a short supply of salt, so the expedition had to take barrels of sugar to use in covering and preserving the fresh beef, which answered the purpose.

Boilvin,[25] the Indian agent at the Prairie, was scared half to death; he acted as British or American, as best answered his purpose. Peter Powell also related that while the negotiations were going on for the surrender at the gate, and the firing had ceased, the Indians pressed up to the outside of the pickets, when one of the Sioux peeping through a crack between the pickets, seeing an American soldier near-by called out "how-do," extending his hand. When the American thrust his hand through between the pickets, the Indian seized it with one hand,

---

[25] For a sketch of Nicolas Boilvin see *Id*, xix, p. 314, note 51.—ED.

at the same time treacherously drawing his knife and cutting the soldier's hand quite to the bone before the treachery was discovered. When Colonel McKay learned the facts, he ferreted out the culprit, and punished him by degrading him to a squaw, depriving him of his gun, and putting on him a petticoat.

Rolette[26] was sent by canoe with a flag and a few men to carry dispatches to Mackinac from Colonel McKay. As they hove in sight of Mackinac, singing their songs, the people all rushed to the landing, asking for news from the expedition before they reached the shore. Rolette, excited and impressed with the importance of what had been accomplished, replied: "Oh, we've gained a great and bloody battle and victory!" when in fact scarcely any lives were lost.

The only Menominee I now recall who served in the War of 1812 and is still living, is Okamawsah, known by the whites as Louis Ducharme. He was a half-breed son of Colonel Ducharme,[27] and on going to parties used to put on his uniform. The Colonel himself was a large, dignified man, and died when quite aged, at Green Bay about 1831.

Tecumseh. From what Souligny and others related, I understand that Tecumseh never visited the Green Bay Menominee in persons; but some of his messengers did come, bringing a wampum belt or speech, urging the Menominee to join the confederacy, and they accomplished their object. Souligny and others had formed a high opinion of Tecumseh, and used to relate that they first saw the great Shawnee leader at Fort Meigs, in the spring of 1813.

Robert Dickson

I know nothing of Dickson's early life. Soon after he came out as a trader, he married a daughter of Wanoti, head chief of the Yankton band of the Sioux—a band that lived on the

---

[26] For Joseph Rolette see *Ibid*, p. 140, note 84.—Ed.

[27] For a brief sketch of Col. Joseph Ducharme, see *Ibid*, p. 293, note 22; his son Louis is mentioned in *Id*, xv, pp. 215–217. Dr. Draper, however, thought that reference was here made to a son of Dominique, brother of Joseph and Paul Ducharme.—Ed.

plains and prairies.[28] His oldest child, William,[29] was in 1819 about twenty-one and just married. Thus he was born about 1798, and Dickson must have formed this marriage connection about 1797. Dickson's wife was a very small woman, fair of complexion, but at forty not handsome. When we left Pembina in the spring of 1822 and went to Fort Snelling, we met Dickson, who shortly after left his children there and took his wife on a visit to England. It was said that he presented her to the king and court, where she maintained herself with much dignity.

The Indians fairly reverenced and worshipped Dickson, regarding him as a great man. He was of fine appearance, over six feet in height, a very large-sized man, in later life being somewhat corpulent, weighing over two hundred pounds. The Indians called him Mascotapah, or The Red-haired Man—sometimes Dick-e-son. He was generous to a fault, and humane. Souligny related that Dickson constantly impressed it upon the Indians not to kill and take scalps when they could take prisoners, saying that the greater warriors took and saved prisoners rather than destroyed them. I also remember having heard that Colonel Snelling entertained Colonel Dickson very courteously at Fort Snelling, in recognition of his humanity during the War of 1812–15.

Dickson used to assure the Menominee and Sioux that those who had served under the British standard should never be forgotten; that their Great Father had empowered him to say that as long as one should be alive who had thus served the king, he should not want; that their lodges should be covered with scarlet cloth.

In 1823 Dickson visited Prairie du Chien, leaving there his daughter Ellen, then a young lady grown, probably to obtain something of an education. This was the last time that I ever saw him. Ellen subsequently married Joseph R. Brown, a sergeant in the army, who was not long after discharged and went

[28] According to Warren, "History of the Ojibwa," in *Minn. Hist. Colls.*, v, p. 363, Wanahta, chief of the Yankton band, was a nephew of Dickson's wife. The former was a noted Sioux chief of the plains of the Red River of the North.—Ed.

[29] For a brief sketch of William Dickson, see *Wis. Hist. Colls.*, xix, p. 444, note 73.—Ed.

to live upon a farm near Fort Armstrong, on the western side of the Mississippi There I once stayed over night with him, and have since learned that he was a member of the Minnesota legislature during its territorial period, so he must have subsequently removed to Minnesota.[30]

Dickson's son Thomas was a clerk in the Indian trade, and got killed in some affray with the Sioux. The younger girl lived at Faribault. I think it was not long after this visit to Prairie du Chien and Green Bay, that the news came of Dickson's death at Drummond Island.[31]

Menominee chiefs

Among the Menominee, the White Beaver (to which Oshkosh belonged), the Wolf, the Turtle, the Crane, and the Bear were the principal clans—there were several lesser ones, such as the Turkey, etc.

Tomah was a large, fine man, much respected by whites and Indians.[32]

Souligny was fond of relating his war exploits, and rather magnified them. He was about five feet nine inches high, very stoutly built, and strong. He died about 1867 of erysipelas, nearly eighty years old, but well preserved.[33]

---

[30] Maj. Joseph R. Brown was one of the most influential of the early settlers of Minnesota. Born in Maryland in 1805, he ran away at the age of fourteen and joined the United States army as a drummer. Coming with Colonel Leavenworth to Fort Snelling in 1819, he was discharged about 1825 and entered the Indian trade. Later he was a pioneer lumberman, printer, legislator, and editor, being the founder of the St. Paul *Pioneer*. He laid out the town of Stillwater, was in both the Wisconsin and Minnesota territorial legislatures, and was one of the best-known men of the region. He died in New York in 1870. See *Minn. Hist. Colls.*, iii, pp. 201-212; iv, p. 41; ix, p. 179.—Ed.

[31] Dickson died at Drummond Island, July 20, 1823, aged fifty-five years.—Ed.

[32] For a brief sketch of this noted chief see *Wis. Hist. Colls.*, xviii, p. 446, note 65; a document in *Id.* xix, p. 346, proves his participation in the War of 1812-15 on the British side.—Ed.

[33] For a different date of Souligny's death see *Id*, x, p. 497—Ed.

Waupomasah, nicknamed Old Sore-Eyes, was principal chief of the Menominee at Lake Shawano. The "Admired Man" is the meaning of his name. He was out in the War of 1812, and died at Keshena about 1868, fully eighty years of age.

Iometah died about the same year that Souligny did—very aged and childish. He was a short, thickset man, about five feet eight inches, an excellent Indian in character.[34]

Poegonah, generally called Big Soldier,[35] died in 1834 or 1835 nearly ninety years of age, at the village of his name in Calumet County, on Lake Winnebago, nearly opposite the mouth of the Black Wolf. From earliest life he had gone on every war expedition with his people, and even with other tribes. Once he was out in a campaign against the Pawnee. He was the tallest man among the Menominee, fully six feet four inches, finely proportioned, and was known for his tall form by all the nations around. He always wore a conspicuous eagle feather on the top of his scalp-lock, so fitted into a small hollow upright bone, with a socket, that it would twirl about with every changing breeze. He seemed to pride himself in having his scalp-lock nicely trimmed and ornamented, as much as to say to his enemies in war, "Come and take it if you can!" But he had an abiding faith that no foe would ever possess it. He attended the treaty at Green Bay in 1828, where a drunken soldier acting as sentinel in protecting the Indian camp, recklessly ran his bayonet through Poegonah's thigh. The old chief seized the soldier, disarmed him with one hand, and grabbing him by the throat with the other, threw him to the ground, calling him a dog, and alleging that if he were an enemy, he would take his life for his insolence. Colonel Brooks, the commanding officer of the troops, had the reckless soldier whipped in the presence of the Indians.[36] Poegonah went out on the Sauk expedition in

[34] See *Ibid*, pp. 497–499, where Dr. Draper gives some additional statements from Powell, with relation to this chief.—Ed.

[35] Compare what Augustin Grignon says of this chief in *Id*, iii, pp. 232, 294.—Ed.

[36] There was no treaty at Green Bay in 1828; Powell doubtless refers to that of 1832, which the Big Soldier signed. At that time, also, Gen. George E. Brooke of the 5th Infantry was commandant at Fort Howard.—Ed.

1832, but said that it was only child's play, although it would serve to give the young warriors some little experience. So in the skirmish near Cassville[37] he did not discharge his gun, but rushed among the combatants to show his fearlessness.

He left two sons, both large men, Sacketook and Wiskeno (or The Bird)—the former was a chief and good Indian. Both have passed away.

Grizzly Bear[38] (Kotskaunoniew), a very large, fleshy Indian, the orator of the Menominee, was smart and intelligent and prided himself on being the white man's friend. He went to Washington with Stambaugh[39] and stayed during the winter of 1830–31. On his return from this trip, where he had been shown everything grand and magnificent, he was asked what had made the most marked impression on his mind. He replied that the grandest sight he had ever witnessed was a large prairie on fire on a dark night—to see the flames jumping and running like lightning, and sending their glare and flashes to the very skies.

When on the Hudson River steamer from New York to Albany, there was quite a large party aboard. Among the number was a fashionable young lady, who expressed to the interpreter a wish to kiss Grizzly Bear, to which that warrior readily assented. When the kiss had been taken and the young lady retired, some of his friends rallied the old chief, saying that the young lady must have fallen in love with him. He replied that that was not her motive—she simply wished to have it to say that she had kissed a brave and noted Indian chief. He had clear ideas of the whites, was of a commanding appearance, and died a few years after the Sauk War, perhaps somewhat more than sixty years of age.

Pewautenot's son Waunako was a pretty smart Indian and a great speaker. He belonged to the band on Menominee River,

---

[37] See *post*.—Ed.

[38] Compare Grignon's account, *Wis. Hist. Colls.*, iii, p. 284; see also *Id*, ii, p. 434. His name in French was *Graisse d'Ours* which signifies Bears' Fat; the denomination "Grizzly" appears to be a misinterpretation—no grizzly bears having had a Wisconsin habitat.—Ed.

[39] Samuel C. Stambaugh was for a short time Indian agent at Green Bay; see *Id*, xi, p. 392; also xii, xv, *passim*.—Ed.

and has been dead several years. The present chief Keshena is his nephew.

Oshkosh[40] possessed, in a remarkable degree, a knowledge of the traditions of his people. He was a man of strong sense and died at Keshena, Shawano County, August 15, 1858. He requested his tribe, when he died, to bury him in a sitting posture, with his pipe, tobacco pouch, gun and powder-horn, and pouch, one beaver steel trap, and a rat trap, so that he might be properly equipped when he arrived in the good hunting ground.

Ahconemay, his oldest son, was to take his place as head chief of the tribe after his death, and he was so considered by the tribe, until he was suspended by the Indian agent for killing Augustin Grignon Jr.[41] Even after his suspension the tribe still regarded him, as they had his father, head chief of the tribe.

Oshkahenawniew, or The Young Man, was Oshkosh's only brother. He was small in stature, abusive and bitter in his speech. He died about 1867, and two of his sons are still living.[42]

Charley Carron is the son of Josette,[43] who was recognized by Governor Cass at the treaty at Little Butte des Morts in 1827 as the second chief of the Menominee. Charley was in my employ as clerk from 1841 until 1845, while I was trading on Fox River, two miles above Omro. When he left my employ he went and settled where Omro now is; he pre-empted the land, but sold out in 1847, and moved to Mukwa on the Wolf River.

---

[40] For this chief see *Id,* iii, iv, *passim.*—Ed.

[41] This event occurred in 1861. Augustin Grignon Jr. was a half-breed son of the elder Augustin, and was employed in the fur-trade. He was killed by Oshkosh's eldest son because he refused to allow him to drink in his cabin. Ahconemay (Aconnamie) was tried and sentenced to state prison; but after a year or more he was pardoned by the governor and returned to the reservation in Shawano County.—Ed.

[42] This chief was about seven or eight years younger than Oshkosh, and took part with the Menominee in most of their activities; see *Wis. Hist. Colls.*, iii, *passim.*—Ed.

[43] Charley Carron, well-educated and of fine physique, was a noted leader of the half-breeds in dare-devil exploits. See R. G. Thwaites, "History of Winnebago County," in Oshkosh *Times* for 1876.—Ed.

He was in the Indian trade at that place until 1854, when he moved to Grand Rapids. While he was in trade he had several narrow escapes from being killed by Indians; was shot at three or four times, and stabbed as many times with a knife. He has stabbed several of the Indians himself. He is still living, spending most of his time at Grand Rapids and Plover on the Wisconsin.

The Indian called The Rubber, I knew well; Augustin Grignon has correctly portrayed him.[44] He was of a boasting disposition, fond of representing himself as a hero of exploits of which no one else had any knowledge; especially claiming to have pre-eminently befriended the Americans and the American cause, when others were aiding the British. This was to gain favor in the eyes of the American military officers, in the shape of a frequent friendly dram. The Rubber was also accustomed to claim gifts from the old settlers at the Bay, on pretence that he was the owner of the territory; but the other Indians would laugh at his pretence to either the ownership of land or to prominence. He died about 1839, somewhere along the shore of Green Bay, perhaps at Grass Point, some eight or nine miles below Green Bay. It was at a time when a large number of the Indians were encamped there with the cholera, and they were prohibited from coming up to Green Bay. Dr. Crane,[45] who yet resides at Green Bay, was employed by the government to attend them, and I used to accompany him on his daily visits as interpreter. The doctor left a quantity of mustard with the Indians, with directions to put a plaster of it over the breast of any one attacked with the disease. The next day when he visited the camp, we were surprised not to see a solitary person stirring anywhere. "Are the poor fellows all dead?" we enquired of each other. But on entering the wigwams, every Indian, old and young, was found spread flat upon his back, covered with a mustard plaster. All had resorted to it, as a precaution against the dread disease, of which large

[44] See *Wis. Hist. Colls.*, iii, pp. 280, 281.—Ed.

[45] The date must have been later, for Dr. C. E. Crane did not settle in Green Bay until 1846. He was born in Ohio, 1827, and died at Green Bay 1897. During the War of Secession he was surgeon for the 5th Wisconsin, and later mayor of his adopted city (1874-79).—Ed.

numbers of them had died—I think The Rubber was among them.

Most of these prominent Menominee chiefs were members of the Catholic church, and the dates of their deaths must be on record at the mission; but there is no priest there now. Maybe the Indian agents kept some record of their deaths; but I hardly think that probable.

As late as 1830, quite a number of Menominee, several chiefs among them, went to Drummond Island[46] and got British presents, guns, traps, brass kettles, ammunition, etc. Col. [George] Boyd, the American Indian agent,[47] on learning of this fact, warned the chiefs that if any of them went there again their medals would be taken away from them, and they would no longer have any claim upon the American government. This firm action on the part of the colonel had the desired effect of breaking off the British influence.

At this time [1877], the tribe numbers about 1350 souls.

Black Hawk War

In 1832, when the Sauk War broke out,[48] General Atkinson[49] sent Col. William S. Hamilton[50] with instructions to the Indian agent, Colonel Boyd, to enlist the Menominee and appoint proper commanding officers. Col. C. S. Stambaugh, who had formerly been connected with the Indian service, and then resided at Green Bay, was selected to command the Menominee, who were 480 in number, divided into companies. Augustin Grignon was captain of one, with Charles A. Grignon his son, for first-lieutenant, and George Grignon his nephew, second-lieut-

[46] For a sketch of the British post on Drummond Island see *Wis. Hist. Colls.*, xix, p. 146, note 94. The post was removed in 1828. For the prolonged British influence over the tribes on American soil see *Id*, xx, *passim*.—Ed.

[47] For this person see *Id*, xii, pp. 266–269.—Ed.

[48] For papers on the Green Bay contingent in the Black Hawk War, see *Id*, iii, pp. 293–295; xii, pp. 217–298.—Ed.

[49] For Gen. Henry Atkinson consult *Id*, i, ii, iv, *passim*.—Ed.

[50] A biographical sketch of William S. Hamilton is given in *Id*, xii, pp. 270, 271.—Ed.

enant. George Johnston commanded the other company, with William Powell first, and Robert Grignon second-lieutenant, while James M. Boyd, a young son of Colonel Boyd, was third-lieutenant and secretary of the company. Alexander Irwin was quartermaster.[51]

We went to Fort Winnebago by land. There Stambaugh received word from General Atkinson of the Bad Axe affair[52] and an order, since the war was now virtually ended, directing him to return to Green Bay and disband the Menominee. The latter were very desirous of going to Prairie du Chien, as they had some relatives and friends residing there, and they probably had some curiosity to go to headquarters and learn all they could about the war. So Stambaugh sent Robert Grignon and me with dispatches to meet Gen. [Winfield] Scott, who was expected at Prairie du Chien, and make known this earnest wish of the Menominee; and say that he would march in that direction. From the Blue Mounds, Grignon returned according to instructions, while I continued on alone to Prairie du Chien, where General Scott had just arrived on board of a steamboat. I delivered to him the dispatches, and he sent me back with dispatches to Stambaugh. Information had just reached General Scott at the very time I appeared, that a hostile party of Sauk and Foxes, said to be a hundred in number, were wending their way down the Mississippi by land. So General Scott concluded to gratify the Menominee and directed Stambaugh and his Indians to repair to Brunet's Ferry, at Little Rock, a few miles above the mouth of the Wisconsin,[53] and thence proceed to intercept those Sauk and Foxes. This permission gratified the Menominee. I overtook the party about

[51] See *Ibid*, p. 278, note 1.—Ed.

[52] See *Ibid*, pp. 257-261.—Ed.

[53] Brunet's Ferry, which for many years has been in disuse, had its southern end in Grant County (section 14, range 6 west, township 6 north), and crossed the Wisconsin in a northwest direction. It was established in 1837 under license from the territorial legislature by Jean Brunet, a French-Canadian of Prairie du Chien, and was on the military road from Fort Winnebago to Fort Crawford. Probably, however, Brunet had lived at this place for some years previous to securing a license, and was in the habit of aiding travellers across the river.—Ed.

forty miles above Prairie du Chien. On reaching Brunet's Ferry, Lieutenant Boyd and I were sent to Prairie du Chien for provisions and any later news about the hostile party. Augustin Grignon is mistaken in saying that Col. William S. Hamilton had anything to do with this expedition, for he had not, and was not along.

Among the Menominee chiefs was Ahkamotte—not La Motte, as Grignon has it—selected by the Indians on this expedition as their prophet, and he held powwows every night to determine where the enemy were.

Colonel Stambaugh with a hundred warriors and six chiefs—Oshkosh, Grizzly Bear, Pewautenot, Souligny, Ahkamotte, and Poegonah—started to pursue the hostiles. They struck the trail and followed it, expecting it would lead to the river not far below the mouth of the Wisconsin; but it bore off from the river. Lieutenants Powell and Boyd, with the remainder of the Indians, some 200 in number, except those sick and sorefooted, were ordered to go direct to the Mississippi and follow its bank, to intercept the enemy should they attempt to cross that river. There were no prominent chiefs with Powell and Boyd; all had gone with Stambaugh, thinking that he would have the expected fight, and reap the honors. Each of these parties kept out spies.

About five miles back of Cassville,[54] in the interior, the next day after leaving Brunet's Ferry in pursuit, they found the enemy camped by a little stream between four and five o'clock in the afternoon. The Sauk and Foxes had had four days the start, but made slow progress, as they had to stop and hunt for their living. The hostiles would keep on the trail for a few miles, then would scatter awhile, then reunite and go on together again. Robert Grignon, Sacketook (son of Poegonah) and two others were in advance spying, and discovered the enemy in a hollow, cooking their venison. They returned and thus reported. The Indians were formed into four parties—one led by Augustin Grignon and the Prophet, with Oshkosh and Poegonah; another party by Robert Grignon; Alexander Irwin led another; and Lieut. C. A. Grignon the fourth. Captain Johns-

[54] The only other printed description of the battle of Cassville known to us, is that of Grignon in *Wis. Hist. Colls.*, iii, pp. 293–295.—Ed.

ton and Colonel Stambaugh remained with the Prophet's party—Johnston because he was somewhat advanced in years.[65]

Just before starting, about half a mile from the hostile camp, Stambaugh made a brief speech to the Indians, saying to them: "Take prisoners. Your Great Father will give you more for one prisoner than he would for a dozen scalps;" and he charged the officers to enforce this order. Grizzly Bear responded in Menominee, Charles A. Grignon interpreting: "Tell our Father here that the Great Spirit saw proper to put a switch in the hands of our Sauk and Fox enemies to chastise us last year, which they did at Prairie du Chien, killing a good many of our people. Now he has seen proper to put that same switch into our hands to-day, which I cannot prevent my young warriors from using. Tell our Father also, that since we left Green Bay we have been obedient children to all his commands; but in this matter about not taking scalps, we must be excused if we fail to regard it."

The Prophet had a large, valuable wampum belt, seven feet long and a foot and a half wide, very heavy; it must have cost fully $70, being made of stone wampum beads, alternately grey and white, from Van Dieman's Land. This was to be the reward for the first scalp to be brought to the Prophet. He also had a flute upon which he was to blow a shrill, loud whistle as a signal for the several parties to raise the war-whoop when they had taken the places assigned them, completely surrounding the enemy. When the signal was given, and the war-whoop raised, they were but a quarter of a mile from the Sauk camp, and it was but a few moments till the whole were rushing down upon them, whooping and hallooing. One of the Sauk fired, but without effect, save to bit off the breech of the gun of Saunapow, or The Ribbon. The latter quickly returned the fire killing him, when several ran to get the scalp; but Saunapow got the main scalp, and others some smaller scalps. Then there was a race for the Prophet, but Saunapow won and received the prize belt, the Prophet keeping the scalp, and thanking the young warrior for a valuable gift. Some of the Sauk women and four or five children seeing that Robert Grignon

[65] For a brief sketch of this person see *Id*, xx.—Ed.

was a white man and approaching the nearest, ran toward him and threw themselves at his feet for protection. Among these was a young warrior, about seventeen years old, who dropped his gun, seeing the hopelessness of the unequal contest, and ran mixing in with the women, and Robert Grignon protected him. Meanwhile some of the Sauk and Foxes ran and hid behind some boulders near by, and one of these was firing from behind a boulder, about half way up the hill, when Grignon started after him, with a Menominee close beside him. The concealed Sauk fired, apparently intending to shoot the Menominee, but the bullet struck Robert Grignon, hitting a rib, and coursed around, lodging in the small of the back. About the same moment Grignon received the fire of another Indian, two buckshot entering his left shoulder. Whereupon the Menominee rushed up and shot the one who first wounded Grignon, killed him, and hacked him up, and kept at him till there was little left of him.

Among the Sauk was a Winnebago with whom some of the Menominee in Calumet had intermarried, and recognized his nationality. He held up his hands and prayed for mercy in the Winnebago language; whereupon a lame Menominee, Okeemonsah, or Little Chief, ran up, and said: "I have been many times to war, and from my lameness was always a little too late; now I will not return without a scalp; you can be no good Winnebago to be with our enemies." Thereupon he gave him a sudden stab with his spear, when he fell, and the Menominee seized his scalp lock, whereupon the Winnebago seized him by the hand on his scalp; but with the free hand Okeemonsah quickly encircled his head, gave him a kick in the back of the neck, and stripped off the scalp, and the poor victim, just after another Menominee had walked up and shot him through the head, soon expired.

Augustin Grignon, naturally very tender-hearted, walked up, and was much touched with such savage conduct; a tear was observed by Grizzly Bear to trickle down Grignon's cheek—Grizzly Bear was an uncommonly large Indian, over six feet, a brawny man, weighing fully 250 pounds. He said to Grignon, "What are you crying for? Was this fellow one of your kindred? If not, you had better go home and join the squaws, who alone indulge in weeping." Grignon gave the old chief a lefthand blow across the mouth, replying that no brave warrior would indulge in such a horrid carnage; that he should be satisfied after having killed his foe; "now", he cried, "since you are so brave a man, resent this, and defend yourself," giving him another blow. But Grizzly Bear, though as well armed as Grignon, refrained from returning blows. Three other Indians were killed in the melee, and a small child on its mother's back was shot through the body between the shoulders, the ball lodging in the mother's clothing. She did not discover that the child was dead, or even hit, till after the affair was over.

The skirmish lasted but a few minutes—the S[illegible] keeping the Menominees at bay by getting behind the rocks and boulders. Eighteen women were taken prisoners, a boy [illegible] years old, and three [illegible] younger children.

Just as the affair was over, Colonel Stambaugh came [illegible] and wished to shake hands with [illegible] Grizzly Bear wanted to know [illegible] the [illegible] hands [illegible]—it was only [illegible] Stambaugh explained [illegible] pleasure at [illegible] scalps.

Boyd and I [illegible] and were approaching to take part. Between the river and the [illegible]-ground, we met four Menominees carrying by hand [illegible] Grignon on a litter of a blanket [illegible] between two poles—meaning to catch an opportunity to get some sort of water conveyance to Prairie du Chien. My [illegible] party then returned to Brunet's Ferry, two Indians taking Grignon up in a canoe which they got from some settlers; and the young Sauk lad, who was taken prisoner, went up with them.

On the way to Brunet's Ferry, my party and Stambaugh's met and went on together, reaching Brunet's the next day. But the night after the fight, Stambaugh and party stopped at a little village where they met General Dodge and Colonel Hamilton, without soldiers, these having been disbanded after the battle of Bad Axe. They got plenty of liquor, for Dodge and Hamilton were treating the Indians freely. The latter indulged in great boasting as to who took the most scalps; by their representation, one would have thought that a great battle had been fought, and hundreds of scalp trophies taken.

After reaching Brunet's Ferry, all the prisoners were assigned to me to convey without any guard to the fort at Prairie du Chien, seven miles distant. When about half way there, I met Wistweaw, the Blacksmith, somewhat in liquor. He was one of those who had conveyed Robert Grignon in a canoe to Prairie du Chien, and approached us begging the privilege of killing the young Sauk and taking his scalp home, so that he could say he had a war trophy—otherwise he would have nothing to relate, only cooking pork and dough-boys. But I refused, saying that the prisoners were confided to me to take and deliver at the fort. Still the Indian plead, and finally made a lunge with his knife at the young Indian who was close to me, but the latter saw the action in time to dodge the blow. Then the Blacksmith was compelled to desist, but ever afterwards he lamented his great misfortune in failing to secure that scalp.

When the news reached Prairie du Chien of the prisoners taken near Cassville, the women of the Menominee band residing at the Prairie, some of whose husbands and brothers had been killed by the Sauk and Foxes the year before, came to Brunet's Ferry, seven miles, to seek revenge. These squaws, to the number of about twenty, arranged themselves on each side of the path. When Stambaugh's party and prisoners crossed at the ferry and landed on the north side, Oshkosh in particular suggested that these Menominee women be examined to see whether they had any weapons with which they could injure the Sauk squaws. Upon search being made, several of them were found to have small tomahawks and knives concealed under their clothing. These were taken from them. But as the Sauk prisoners passed between the rows of Menominee women, the latter availed themselves of an Indian custom for each to touch the prisoners as they passed. Some barely touched them tenderly with the tips of their fingers, while others seized them by their hair and shook and jerked them about without mercy. The Sauk women were rejoiced to get off without worse treatment. They were kept in duress a short time in the garrison at Prairie du Chien, then sent down to Rock Island, and soon after discharged.

After a few days of recruiting and preparation, the Menominee returned home, scattering from Butte des Morts. Robert Grignon remained some time in the hospital at Prairie du Chien. Doctor Beaumont[56] easily extracted the buckshot from his shoulder; but the ball in his back could not with safety be taken out. Grignon drew a pension of $15 per month and lived till he froze to death, near his own house, not far from Christmas, about twelve years ago.[57]

Makata Mishekakah, or the Black Falcon, was the name the Sauk and Foxes gave Col. Zachary Taylor. Aheheechawk, or the White Crane, was their name for General Scott. Black Hawk claimed that he surrendered himself, as he had heard that in case he did so, all the prisoners would be released. On reaching Prairie du Chien, Colonel Taylor brought out handcuffs to put on him. "Why do you want to put the handcuffs on me when I have given myself up and can't get away; I had expected better treatment from the Black Falcon." Taylor replied that it was not his wish to do so, and that he was sorry so to treat him; but he was himself but a small chief, and had to obey the orders of his superiors; and these were the orders of the big chief, the White Crane. Then Black Hawk said that he had supposed the Black Falcon was too humane to treat him thus; but as these were the orders of the White Crane, then do so—whereupon he extended his hands and received the handcuffs.

At the treaty at Rock Island, General Scott had Black Hawk degraded from his chieftainship and Keokuk appointed in his place. Keokuk rose and addressed Black Hawk, saying that this was not of his own seeking, that he regretted Black Hawk's degradation; but the latter had, contrary to his advice, plunged himself and people into the war, and the Great Father had taken the chieftainship from him. Then Black Hawk addressed General Scott, asking why he who had not conferred this honor upon him, could have the power to deprive him of it. Pointing

---

[56] For Dr. William Beaumont see *Id*, xv, p. 397, note 4.—Ed.

[57] Robert Grignon was the eldest son of Pierre Antoine, himself the eldest of the Grignon brothers. Robert was born about 1804 at Green Bay. He early entered the fur-trade, and was a clerk for his uncles, settling first at Butte des Morts, later within the limits of Oshkosh. He died in 1864, frozen near his own home, having become bewildered in a storm.—Ed.

his finger upward, he indicated that the One who had made him a chief alone could unmake him.

Capt. William Powell

When my father returned from Hudson Bay in 1822 and left me in the care of Captain Alexander, I remained with him three years at Fort Snelling. The captain being sent on a recruiting service to St. Louis, took me with him, and during his stay there sent me to school five miles from Belle Fontaine.

I remained there until the spring of 1827, when I came to Rock Island, and stayed until the first of September, 1828, when my father sent for me and I came home to Butte des Morts. When I arrived where Portage City now is, Major Twiggs had just got there with two or three companies of United States troops to commence building the fort, which was called Fort Winnebago.[58] Twiggs was the commanding officer. Jefferson Davis[59] was also there, just from West Point; he was only second-lieutenant at that time.

Two years later, while Lieutenant Davis was stationed at Fort Winnebago, Twiggs still commanding, a powerful Kentuckian named Stewart, a carpenter by trade, dwelt there as Daniel M. Whitney's agent in transporting boats over the portage. There was a camp of Menominee Indians near the American Fur Company's store, where Pierre Paquette lived,[60] and Stewart went over one day with a tanned deer skin to get some moccasins made. It was a Sunday, and Davis happening to be there, ordered him off. Stewart intimated that he had as much right there as Davis had, and that he should go when he got ready, and not before. Davis felt his dignity insulted, and gave Stewart an unexpected and heavy blow. Stewart recovering, pitched upon Davis and gave him a severe whipping, badly bruising his face and eyes. I was then a clerk in the store, and Davis had me get a chicken, kill it, and put the fresh carcass on

---

[58] See account of this event and a sketch of Twiggs in *Wis. Hist. Colls.*, xiv, pp. 65–76.—ED.

[59] On Davis at Fort Winnebago see *Ibid*, pp. 72–75; also *Id*, viii–x, xii, xiii, *passim*.—ED.

[60] For an account of Pierre Paquette see *Id*, vii, pp. 382–385.—ED.

his face, to prevent the [illegible] having their discolored marks. Stewart himself [illegible] by Mr. Whitney, his employer, [illegible] lest he should be retaliated on by [illegible] and he subsequently returned to Kentucky.

Except for a short time [illegible] I remained with my father at Butte des Morts [illegible] went as first-lieutenant in the Black Hawk War. [illegible] war, I returned home and went into partnership [illegible] Grignon in the Indian trade. We established our trading post at Algoma in the fall of 1832, and continued at that place till the fall of 1835, when we dissolved our copartnership and I went and lived with my father until he died.

Treaties. I was appointed United States interpreter for the Menominee in 1836. The same year, Gov. Henry Dodge of Mineral Point was appointed commissioner to make a treaty with the Menominee; this was concluded September 3, 1836.[61] After the treaty I resigned and went into the Indian trade on Fox River, two miles above where Omro now is, and continued to trade there till 1846, when for a year I established a trading post at the mouth of Shawano Creek, in Shawano County. Then quitting the Indian trade, I was again appointed, in 1848, United States interpreter and in that capacity served at the treaty of that year. Medill was the commissioner on the part of the Government in that treaty, wherein the Menominee ceded all of their country that they owned in Wisconsin for $400,000. By its terms the Government gave them for their future home a tract of 500,000 acres of land on the Crow Wing River,[62] 150 to 200 miles above St. Paul. They were to remain in Wisconsin for two years after the ratification of the treaty, and then to move to the Crow Wing. At the same time the Government agreed to furnish $5,000 to defray the expenses of a delegation of nine chiefs with their head chief Oshkosh to go and examine the country, before removing in 1850.

Visit to Washington. President Taylor instructed Major Bruce, Indian agent at Green Bay, to take a delegation of chiefs

---

[61] Powell was sworn interpreter at the Menominee treaty of 1836.—Ed.

[62] The treaty guaranteed that there should not be less than 600,000 acres of land in the tract assigned.—Ed.

and go and survey the land alloted them on the Crow Wing, and after doing so to bring the same delegation to Washington and report. I accompanied the delegation to the Crow Wing, and with us went my old friend Charles Tullar,[63] who was employed to survey the tract. He did not, however, go on with us to Washington, as he had more important business that required him to remain at Green Bay. Arriving at Washington on September 4 we remained there some two weeks before Oshkosh with the other chiefs could get an interview with the commissioner of Indian affairs. There were at the federal capital representatives of several other tribes of Indians, who had business with their great father, the president, who had got there some days ahead of us; so we had to wait till our turn came. When the time arrived, our Wisconsin chiefs were notified that they might come and see their great father and talk over their business with him. We conducted Chief Oshkosh and the rest of the Indians to the commissioner's office at about 9 o'clock A. M. Here we were received by Chief-clerk Charles E. Mix, acting in the place of the commissioner, Mr. Lowrey, who was sick at the time. After a short talk, Mr. Mix accompanied the delegation to the office of the secretary of the interior, and from there the latter conducted his visitors to the White House. After the chiefs were seated according to rank, President Fillmore, accompanied by General Scott, entered and the chiefs were presented and shook hands with both. Chief Oshkosh recognized General Scott, for he had seen him both at Green Bay and at the treaty at Prairie du Chien. The general also recollected Oshkosh, who was a small man, standing only about five feet. When he shook hands with the general, Oshkosh said: "You are like a tall pine tree, and myself like a scrub-oak, so I stand under your branches to protect my head from harm."

The interview with their Great Father was brief. Oshkosh

[63] Charles Tullar was born in 1804 in Vermont. Coming to Green Bay in 1830, he entered the employ of Daniel Whitney and was occupied in lumbering, mining, surveying, etc. He acted as sheriff for Brown County, 1836-43. He was accustomed to say that the happiest days of his life were spent with William Powell, his close friend, surveying Indian reservations. The latter years of his life were employed as agent for the Whitney estate. He died at Green Bay Oct. 20, 1874.—ED.

stated in a very few words that the Crow Wing country was not what it had been represented to his tribe by Commissioner Medill, who made the treaty of 1848; and that the tribe did not like to move to that country because the Indians already there were continually engaged in intertribal war. He preferred, he said, a home somewhere in Wisconsin, for the poorest region in Wisconsin was better than that of the Crow Wing. He said that the latter was a good country for the white man, for he was numerous and could protect himself from those warlike tribes; but his own tribe was small, and he wished them to live in peace for the little time they had to live.[64]

The latter part of September I started from Washington for Green Bay in charge of the delegation, and was instructed by the department to stop at the largest Eastern cities a few days and show the chiefs the principal places so as to give them an idea how numerous their white brothers were. We stayed a week in New York and went to Barnum's Museum every day. Barnum invited Oshkosh and his chiefs to come and hear the great singer Jenny Lind, but Oshkosh declined the invitation. A few of the younger chiefs went, however, but when they were asked by the other chiefs how they liked the singing, they replied that she made a very big noise and then a little noise. The white man must have a great deal more money than he needed, to pay so much to hear this lady sing.

Henry Merrell errs in giving the name of Powell, the trader at Green Lake, as William.[65] His first name was James, and he was a cousin of mine. He came to Green Bay about 1833, and engaged in the Indian trade; in 1838 he moved west of the Mississippi, into Iowa, and I have since lost track of him.

---

[64] Permission was given to the Menominee to remain in Wisconsin, which was afterwards confirmed by the treaty of 1854, assigning them a reservation in Shawano County.—Ed.

[65] See *Wis. Hist. Colls.*, vii, p. 387.—Ed.

John B. Dubay

John B. Dubay[66] was son of a Canadian, whose name I think was Louis.[67] He came here early; his first wife was a Menominee woman, daughter of the principal chief on the Menominee River, named Pewatenot, and mentioned in Grignon's "Narrative" as serving in the War of 1812. He also had a son Louis, who was only a *voyageur*. J. B. Dubay was at least four years older than myself, certainly being born as early as 1806. When a young man, he became a successful trader among the Chippewa. When he went among the Indians, he would pitch his large markee, fit it up neatly with folding seats and a showy carpet, and invite the Indians there. Its attractive appearance would fix their attention, they would feel honored by the attention and would be quite sure to give him their trade. Dubay was known to them as Oskaatawananee, or the Flourishing Young Trader.

In the early years of the Territory and State, he was fond of going to Madison, where he spent his money freely, and would send off to borrow more. Once he borrowed of me while I was clerk in a store of the American Fur Company in which Dubay had an interest. I subsequently asked him what his business was, there. "Why," said he, "I am a *log* member"—meaning a lobby member; he liked to boast that his company at the capital included prominent lawyers, judges, and legislators.

Once I was reminding him that he had neglected to be present at a certain Chippewa treaty and secure his claim for credits to Indians. "Oh," he replied, "I shall not be too late, for the payments have not all been paid; they are to be paid," he said, "in *storn*"—meaning in installments. He had, he said, sent his *monster* (remonstrance) to the Indian department, and he would be all right. But he lost it. He was fond of trying to repeat big words, but would invariably make ridiculous work of it.

---

[66] See *Ibid*, pp. 391, 400-402. This statement of Powell is an addition to and correction of Merrell's narrative concerning Dubay, and Draper's statement in a note that he was born in 1810.—Ed.

[67] The name was originally Dubée. Louis was living in Green Bay as late as 1836.—Ed.

Dubay had a fine appreciation of Indian character. He knew well how to gain the confidence and the patronage of his red brethren, and thus acquired a considerable influence over them. Had he had a good education, he would have made his mark in the world.

In killing Reynolds, he was advised by lawyers that he had rights that he should protect, and he thought he was doing only what was justifiable. But he was naturally a high-toned, generous-hearted man; and when he came to reflect that he had taken the life of a fellow man, though acquitted of criminal intent, it preyed upon his mind, and he has never since been the man he was before. He now (1877) resides above Stevens Point.

Origin and Meaning of Indian Names

Ashkeoton (town, Brown Co.)—The Crier, name of an Indian.

Assippun, or Ashippun (town, Dodge Co.)—The Raccoon.

Brulé (river, Douglas Co.)—Burnt timber; Indian word Wesaucota, in both Menominee and Chippewa.

Buffalo (lake, Marquette Co.)—Pesahkeoconnee, a great buffalo range in early times. I never saw any buffalo in Wisconsin, nor have the oldest Menominee in their day. Iometah and others used to say that their fathers killed and drove them off.

Butte des Morts (lake and town, Winnebago Co.)—Pahquatenohsah was the Indian word for Little Butte des Morts, meaning small mound of the dead. Maspahquatenoh is big mound of the dead—"noh" meaning dead.

Embarrass (river, tributary to Wolf)—Indian word was Ok-[illegible] Saparo, or floating wood. The French adopted this and called it *La Rivière s'embarrass* (the river that is "embarrassed," or interrupted, by driftwood).

Kekoskee (town, Dodge Co.)—Of Winnebago origin.

Keshena (town, Shawano Co.)—The Scudding Cloud, named after a Menominee chief yet living, son of Josette, second chief, and son-in-law of Pewatenot.

Kewaskum (town, Washington Co.)—Name of a Menominee Indian, The Turner: one who has power as a medicine man to turn things as he pleases.

Kewaunee (county and town)—A specie of duck.

Koshkonong (town, Rock Co.)—Not Menominee; probably Potawatomi in origin.

Manitowoc (county and town)—Place of spirits.

Markesan (village, Green Lake Co.)—Probably a Winnebago word.

Maskee—Indian word for marsh.

Mazomanie (town, Dane Co.)—Place of iron deposits, a Winnebago word.

Meeme (town, Manitowoc Co.)—The Pigeon.

Menominee—thus Captain Powell spells the name. The plural is Omahnominewowk, or Wild Rice People, as they call themselves. They still harvest wild rice in Shawano Lake and other lakes above, but do not use it to the same extent as formerly.

Mishicott (town, Manitowoc Co.)—Hairy Leg.

Mukwonago, or Maquonigo (town, Waukesha Co.)—Of Potawatomi origin.

Nashotah (town, Waukesha Co.)—Twin, a Potawatomi word.

Necedah (town, Juneau Co.)—Winnebago word.

Neosho (town, Dodge Co.)—Either Winnebago or Potawatomi word.

Neshkoro (town, Marquette Co.)—Winnebago word.

Oconomowoc (county and town)—Probably Potawatomi.

Oconto (county and town)—The place of the pickerel.

Okee (town, Columbia Co.)—Winnebago word.

Ozaukee (county)—The Sauks.

Packwaukee, or Pakwaukea (town, Marquette Co.)—The Mound, a natural elevation.

Pensaukee (river and town, Oconto Co.)—The place of the brant—a species of small wild geese.

Peshtigo, properly Pasheteco (town, Marinette Co.)—Passing through the marsh.

Powaaconnee—Poygan abbreviated.

Poygan (lake, Winnebago Co.)—The threshing place (for rice).

Poynette (town, Columbia Co.)—Perhaps of Winnebago origin.

Poysippi (town, Waushara Co.)—Same as Poygan, with *sippi*, (meaning river) added.

Puckaway (lake, Green Lake Co.)—Cat Tail Flag.

Shawano (lake and county)—South; the county was named from the lake: Shawano, or South, Lake. I could not learn from the Menominee how this name was derived. Oshkosh once said to me that his ancestors told him a prophet from the South visited the Menominee, and first made his appearance at the Shawano Lake, proclaiming himself a prophet from the South; that he was going to change things generally, to reform their medical remedies and reform their government, and then they would live much longer. I am satisfied, since it has been explained to me about Tecumseh's brother the Prophet, that he was the one who came to the Menominee about 1810 and aimed at their reform; and that he was the one whom Oshkosh referred to and described.

Sheboygan (county and town)—Properly Chapewyaconnee, a Menominee word, meaning a rumbling subterranean sound, as if it were a spirit sound, heard in the lake at the mouth of the river, at that point. Solomon Juneau used to state to me that it was a Potawatomi word, and meant the place of the mermaid.

Suamico (river, Brown Co.)—Red Sand River.

Taycheedah (town, Fond du Lac Co.)—A Winnebago name.

Wauconsta (town, Fond du Lac Co.)—Not a Menominee word.

Waukesha, or Waukeshoon (county and town)—Something about a fox.

Waupaca (river, county, and town)—The dawning of the morning. The French endeavored to give the meaning by calling it To-Morrow River.

Waupun (town, Fond du Lac Co.)—Day-break or dawn.

Waushara (county)—A Winnebago word.

Wautoma (town, Waushara Co.)—Not a Menominee word.

Wauseka (town, Crawford Co.)— A Winnebago word.

[illegible] (town, Winnebago Co.)—A Winnebago word.

Weyauwega (town, Waupaca Co.)—Named by Judge Doty after an Indian Weauwega, said to have lived there and claimed the country. But others said that the name of the locality came from Weyawaea, the grand encampment, as it was a noted Indian camping place. This latter seems to me most probable.

Winneconne (town, Winnebago Co.)—The place of the skull, a battleground, where some of the Sauk and Foxes were chased by the French and Menominee at the Butte des Morts battle. See *ante*, p. 150.

Wyocena (town, Columbia Co.)—A Winnebago word.

Pioneers and Durham Boats on Fox River

By John Wallace Arndt[1]

The site on which the present city of Green Bay is built, was in 1824 covered with a forest of many kinds of trees and much underbrush, with here and there a bit of swamp. A narrow strip of grassland, about two hundred feet in width, extended from what is now Main Street along the river shore to the slough near Doty Street. The east side of what is now Washington Street

[1] John Wallace Arndt, son of John P. Arndt, a well-known early innkeeper of Green Bay, was born at Wilkesbarre, Pa., Sept. 15, 1815. At the age of nine, John Wallace Arndt removed with his father to Green Bay, there attending school and assisting his father in transporting goods on the Fox River of Wisconsin. In 1834 he went to school in the East and was for a time at Yale College. He studied law with his brother Charles, but never was admitted to the bar, and settled in De Pere, where his homestead is still standing. In 1842 he married Mary C., daughter of Randall Wilcox. Arndt died at De Pere Jan. 12, 1897. In 1894 he published a pamphlet entitled *The Early History of Green Bay and the Fox River Valley. Personal Reminiscenses.* From this pamphlet, privately printed and now rare, we extract and greatly condense the following narrative, which has several points of excellence: its intimate account of the introduction to Wisconsin waters, in 1825, of the Durham boat, invented in 1750 by Robert Durham of Bucks County, Pa.—for further details of this craft see R. G. Thwaites (ed.), *Early Western Travels* (Cleveland, Ohio, 1904-07), ix, p. 323; its glimpses of several important pioneer settlers in the Fox River valley; its detailed description of the interesting old Pierre Grignon house at Green Bay; and its graphic chronicle of a typical voyage of a Durham boat from Green Bay to Fort Winnebago (Portage) and return, in 1830.—Ed.

John P. Arndt (1780-1861)

From oil portrait by Samuel M. Brookes, in possession of the Society

corresponds with the line where the woods and the grass met. This strip was a favorite camping ground for the Indians.

A man by the name of Kelso had built a small log house, which he used as a dwelling and store, on the lots where the Cook House now stands. He afterwards moved to Wrightstown. There was no other building or evidence of any, north of the slough, except the remains of a shabbily-built barn made of small, round poles, near the foot of Doty Street.

The road between Green Bay and De Pere began at the slough and followed the trend of the river, passed west of Pierre Grignon's old house, and then about twenty feet east of John P. Arndt's dwelling. It then passed to the west of Judge Lawe's place, following the bank of the river on the same track where the railroad is now, until it struck the high land below Louis Grignon's house, where it turned up into the present road, and so on to De Pere.

Destruction of an Old House

Pierre Grignon's old house stood near the intersection of Stuart and Washington streets, about two-hundred feet south of the slough, and the same distance from Fox River.[2] It fronted the west, was fifty feet square and one-and-a-half stories high, with its gables north and south. It was built of pine logs, hewn and dressed with the plane, until they lay flat 10x12 inches. In laying up this timber the workmen had nicely dovetailed each corner, making a very close joint—in fact, this was the case throughout the building, great pains having apparently been taken to do the work well.

The roof was very steep, covered with cedar bark, now nearly six inches thick. There were many layers of the cedar covering,

[2] This seems to have been the house that Pierre Grignon built, described as follows by his son Augustin in *Wis. Hist. Colls.*, iii, p. 253: "When my father erected a new house, about 1790, he had to send to Montreal for a carpenter and mason; his house was a hewed log building, and at that time was regarded as altogether the best at Green Bay." It was probably in this house that Pierre Grignon's widow (Madame Langevin) died in 1823. See references to this place in *Id*, xx, *passim*.—Ed.

showing that it had frequently been repaired without removing the old bark.

The upper floor was supported by heavy beams, 12x14 inches in size, crossing the building east and west, four feet apart, and dressed with an inch bead worked on the lower corners. The floors were all made of two-inch pine plank, dressed, plowed, and grooved. All of the partitions were dressed in the same way, but on both sides. There were two chimneys, one on each gable, built of limestone and flush with the outside of the timbers, showing the stone from top to base. The fireplaces were high and broad, projecting well into the room, and could easily take in a four-foot log.

The first floor of the house was divided into four rooms besides a vestibule, in the following manner: A 25x30 feet room was in the southwest corner; on the east side of this large room were two bedrooms, 15x15 feet square, opening into it. The kitchen was a large room in the northeast corner, with a door opening to the east, also an inner door entering the vestibule on the west side. The main entrance to the house was through this vestibule, in the northwest corner, where also was the stairway and a door leading into the large front room. In this latter room was one of the fireplaces, also two triangular closets, one in its northeast, and the other in the southwest corner, made of pine; each with four doors, two below and two above. The two upper doors of each closet were ornamented with a carving in demi-relief, representing the royal insignia of France—the *fleur-des-lis*. How meritorious the carving was when first made, I cannot tell. It was not protected with paint or varnish; old age had dimmed its outlines and dulled its sharp relief. Yet there was enough left to show what it was intended to represent. It is a pity these doors were lost, for they never can be duplicated.

Over the main entrance of the house was a portico, which showed considerable artistic taste and skill. The windows were but few and small. The upper story was without divisions, save the supports of each rafter; there were two windows in the north gable, on each side of the chimney.

This old house with its surroundings and the farm on which it stood, plainly showed the intelligence and enterprise of the man who planned and built it. Across the road, west of the house, stood the store, a well-constructed building, 20x30, two stories high. Nearer the river, a few rods west, were the ruins of another building, probably a storehouse. About fifty feet north of the house was a building larger than the store, built in the same style as the house, two stories high, and divided into two rooms, which undoubtedly were used for storing grain and provisions. A large square garden of about two acres southeast of the house was enclosed by a fence beginning at the southwest corner, running south on a line with the house, then turning east and north—the north fence meeting the house near its middle on the east side. The fence was seven or eight feet high, built of cedar posts eight feet apart, a rabbet being made on each side of the post, and shakes of cedar filled the space; a cap or coping was secured on top with tenon and mortise. North of the house, and on a line with the west front, was a fence similar to that of the garden and extending to the slough. In this fence and close to the house was placed a large gateway, with a smaller one on the side, through which the road passed to the barns at the east.

A few rods east of the garden was a large barn which stood with its gables north and south, nearly a hundred feet long, thirty feet wide, and eighteen or twenty feet to the plate, with three bays, two threshing floors, and four sets of double doors. It was built entirely of cedar except the roof, which was made with tamarack poles and thatched with straw. The same plan was used as in building the garden fence, only the timber was much larger; massive cedar trees were used for posts, but set farther apart, the plates and other timber used being much larger. It was an immense barn; I think it would have stored five or six hundred tons of hay, and remained standing several years after we moved here.

About a hundred feet east of the barn, and at a right angle, was the horse and cow stable, built in the same fashion as the home buildings, of hewn pine but thatched with straw. Around these buildings was the accumulation of forty years or more of rotten straw and manure, covering more than an acre and in some places four or five feet thick. It took father a long time to remove and spread it on the farm, a part of which he rented and cultivated many years. The cleared and cultivated part of the farm at that time extended from a point a little north of

Doty Street south to Judge Lawe's north line, and east to Van Buren Street and Webster Avenue.

Before we leave the old house and garden, so familiar to me in early youth, I will relate my connection with it. In 1825 father rented the garden, together with the farm, and from that time to the platting of Astor he used it for his family. Here I served my apprenticeship in gardening. The house being much out of repair, was used only at short intervals during the summer and by a worthless set, which caused some sacrilegious person to dub it the "Nunnery." Over on Duck Creek, where he spent his winters, making shingles and cutting cord wood, was a discharged soldier named Marsdon, who was married to a squaw; when a white man took a squaw to wife he took the whole family, sisters, brothers-in-law, aunts, and cousins. In summer, Marsdon and his numerous family moved to the city, the females not liking the loneliness of rural life. Without leave or license they took possession of this old house.

This sounded the knell of the once grand old house. Father purchased it with the privilege of tearing it down. My brother Charles and I, with men to help us, began the work of destruction. Our plan was first to remove the supports to the roof, as far as we thought it safe to the workmen; then we undermined the chimneys, so that when the roof fell it would carry them with it. This part of the work being done we awaited the result. The roof being covered with so many layers of cedar bark, had become rotten and porous and absorbed water like a sponge. In a few days a storm came, a regular northeaster; the wind blew and the rain poured on that devoted roof, and in the darkness of night the crash came, carrying destruction with it. The ruin was complete; nothing remained standing but a part of the outside walls.

Could these walls have spoken, they would have told of deliberate councils held within, debating the chances of peace or war, of trade and commerce. They would have told of festive scenes, the table loaded with fish, flesh, and fowl, gathered by the hunters' skill from the river, lake, and forest. They would have told, too, of music and the dance, so dear to the gay and festive Frenchmen. Thither came native chiefs and warriors; white men also, for trade and profit; others for the mere love of exploration—men wise in council, strong in war, who led that host of savages who surprised and defeated Braddock.[3]

American Pioneers

In 1824, when father first landed on the shores of Fox River,[4] he was just forty-two years old, in full health and strength of body and mind, well equipped for the labor he wished to undertake. From the early age of eighteen years, until his father's death (in 1802) he had been connected with him in business—milling, lumbering, merchandizing, and other occupations, such as building Durham boats. The last-named industry made a large and for many years a successful business. Grandfather Arndt was a shrewd and intelligent man; he knew how to make money, how to keep and to use it. His firm took the lead in Wilkesbarre, Luzern County, Pennsylvania. After his death, his only son and heir was my father, who took full control of the business and was successful until the crisis of 1815–16, and its crash. Thus he brought with him to this region the experience of more than twenty years of business success and failure.

Father was much interested in the navigation and improvement of the Fox and Wisconsin rivers. The project was much discussed among the few leading business men—James Doty, Daniel Whitney, the two Irwin brothers, John Lawe, the Grignons, and some others. This was the beginning of the Fox River Company, to demonstrate the feasibility of freighting on the Fox River in its natural state, in a reasonable time, and at a fair profit.

In the spring of 1825 father built the first Durham boat, equipped and loaded it with a stock of goods for Fever River (now Galena), where a store was opened, The plan was to purchase lead, and transport it to Green Bay by the way of the Wisconsin and Fox rivers, thereby opening another outlet for the lead to the Eastern market.

---

[3] Referring to the well-known tradition that Charles Langlade, father-in-law of Pierre Grignon, led the Indians in the fatal attack on Braddock in 1755—many years, however, before this house was built.—ED.

[4] For a brief biographical sketch of John P. Arndt see *Wis. Hist. Colls.*, xx.—ED.

This business was put in charge of a man by the name of Abbot, a good business man, one who knew all about Durham boats. He had been in father's employ at Wilkesbarre for many years. After a year's trial the project was given up, the whole difficulty being in navigating the Wisconsin; the Fox was all right. Though the first attempt was a partial failure, nothing daunted, the boat building went on.

Treaty of Butte des Morts

In 1827 a commission was appointed, headed by Lewis Cass, governor of Michigan. The commissioners located the treaty at Little Butte des Morts, just where the Chicago & Northwestern railroad turns on the west bank to cross Lake Butte des Morts to Menasha. This had been a favorite cemetery for the Indians, but most of it has since been removed to make room for the railway. At the time of the excavations, many curiosities were found, such as stone and copper axes, arrow heads, spears or lance heads, and heaps of bones. In preparation for the treaty, there was planted on the apex of this mound a tall flag-staff, from which floated the stars-and-stripes.

The buildings for the governor and his suite were placed near the mound, while the camps of the different tribes were situated some distance from headquarters. Those natives friendly to one another were by themselves; those disposed to be quarrelsome were placed apart from the peaceful, for fear some old feud might be revived. The Indian neither forgets nor forgives.

These small native encampments presented a novel sight to the stranger, in the neatness with which they were built, and the ingenuity displayed in the use of scant material. A few small poles stuck in the ground were covered with rush mats or dressed skins, a hole being left in the top for the smoke to escape. Such wigwams were warm, comfortable, and dry. It was a unique sight, this city built almost in a day on the banks of a beautiful lake, surrounded by the primeval forest sweeping around it in a circle three or four miles deep. There were tribes from the north and south, the east and the west, speaking their various tongues and dressed each in their peculiar costumes. And in their center was the flag-staff.

Pioneers and Durham Boats on Fox River

Robert Irwin and my father had obtained the contract for furnishing and delivering on the treaty grounds all provisions, together with all necessary buildings, including quarters for the governor and suite, which numbered in all about eighty persons. The contractors furnished beds and bedding, chairs, tables with their crockery and glassware. The food and luxuries necessary to satisfy this motley crowd were a wonder to behold. The quantity was considerable, and in quality the best that the government money could purchase. Of liquor there was also an abundant store, both from still and press.

In securing the contract with the United States, Irwin was the political power behind the throne; but father was equipped for the business in material and appliances, and a thorough knowledge of the situation. His boats furnished the transportation, and his saw-mill the lumber for the treaty buildings. The goods and supplies were stored in his warehouse at Green Bay, and prepared for transportation to the treaty ground. In this undertaking the Durham boats were in constant use, and people wondered at the ease with which they seemed to solve the problem of navigating the Fox.

Description of the Durham Boat

The Durham boat had long been used on the Delaware and Susquehanna rivers, which are somewhat similar to the Fox, being interrupted by rapids and shallow water. The boat was of simple build, carrying a large load with light draft, and passing easily through the water. Generally they were from forty-five to sixty feet in length, ten to twelve feet beam, two and one-half feet deep, drawing eighteen to twenty inches, and carrying from twenty-five to thirty tons of freight.

The bottom was constructed of $1\frac{1}{2}$ inch oak plank, with one streak above the bend; above this to the gunwale, pine was used. The timbers of the frame were of oak, $3x3\frac{1}{2}$ inches, steamed and bent, or worked out of natural crooks; oak beams 4x5 inches were placed athwart the boat eight or nine feet apart, and made to crown or arch four or five inches. The waist began about eight feet from the stern and extended perfectly straight to within eight feet of the bow. The sheer began at these two points, fore and aft, raising the stem and stern a few inches above the waist. The boat was sharp at both ends, which were decked over to the waist, where the walking board began, and ran the whole length of the waist. The walking board was about fourteen inches wide; combings 2x4 inches were secured to the inner side to give it strength and increase the freeboard.

For the first boats that father built, he had much trouble and expense in procuring the right kind of lumber. They required plank from twenty to thirty feet long, both pine and oak. His mill was not yet arranged to saw such long lumber, so he resorted to the whip saw. The timber was cut the proper lengths, hewn on two sides, and by the use of two men and a whip saw made into lumber. However, as the demand for boats increased, he soon remedied this lack. He built boats not only for his own use but for other parties; several for the American Fur Company, Daniel Whitney, and others. The manufacture of these craft soon grew into a large business, and gave employment to many men; it continued until the improvement of the Fox River commenced.

The steering oar was the novelty of the boat, hewn from a pine tree twenty feet long and large enough to make a blade twelve inches wide and three or four feet long. The pivotal point was about eleven feet from the end of the blade; the stock so arches to this point that when the boat was loaded the handle of the oar would be three feet above the deck. At this pivotal point a slotted mortise was made to receive a 1½ inch iron pin driven into the head of the stern post, on which to hang the oar. The oar was now put in place, dressed and thinned until it was in balance, so that it would work easily in all necessary directions. The principal propelling power was the socket pole, with a good, strong man at the other end of it. This pole was made of the best and toughest white ash fifteen feet long, 1¾ inches in its largest part, and tapering to 1½ inches at the top, on this being placed a button, to ease the pressure on the shoulder. The pocket was of iron, armed with a square steel point, well-tempered and kept sharp. The ordinary oar was seldom used, although one for each man was provided in case of need. A mast, sail, and oilcloths were a part of the outfit, beside a heavy block and tackle and a long tow-line. Thus equipped the boat was a complete innovation at the time of its introduction on the Fox River.

The French trader with his bateau drawing over two feet of water, carrying ten or twelve tons of freight, propelled with oars or small hand poles by a crew of ten or twelve men, who stopped every three miles to smoke their pipes and rest, looked on this big boat with doubting eyes. "It is too big," "Cannot get her over the rapids," "Takes too many men," "Costs too much"—such were the criticisms. That long oar perched upon the stern gave them much trouble and anxiety. "Oh! you will soon take that thing off the stern and put two or more Frenchmen with their small handy poles there, to steer your boat." It was knowledge perfected by experience against ignorance and prejudice. The prophets failed. The Durham boat won the prize and kept it until the river was improved and the steamboat took its place.

A Trip on the Fox River

The time chosen to make this imaginary trip will be in the month of June, 1830. By that time the transportation business was well-established and systematized. We had learned the best, quickest, most economical way in which to conduct it. Our men were drilled and understood their work. I had this season been promoted to the captaincy of my first boat, with all the power, emoluments, and honors that that position gave. Although a few years later I was appointed captain of a militia company belonging to Col. Samuel Ryan's regiment, I think I was prouder of my first command than of my second. The boatmen were better drilled than the soldiers, and I knew more about running a boat than a militia company.

Let us go to John P. Arndt's warehouse, standing on Point Pleasant on the riverside fronting his dwelling, and see how the goods were prepared for transportation. As they had to be handled a number of times in transit, rolled or carried over rough and difficult places on ladders placed along the shore, it was necessary to have the packages of such weight that two or three men could handle them easily without breakage or damage, thereby saving both time and money. The freightage being paid by the hundred pounds, we paid the teamster in the same way for hauling the goods over the portage. Therefore it became necessary to weigh each package and mark thereon the weight. They were then checked on the wagons and a receipt given of the weight of each load, to avoid any misunderstanding.

The boat is to be loaded today, so that we can make an early start tomorrow morning, thus arriving at the Grand Kaukauna landing a couple of hours before dark. Seven men compose my crew, for my boat is large and heavily loaded. Six is the ordinary crew, beside the captain or steersman. Everything is ready, cast off the lines and let her go. Each pole is quickly set, the button placed on the big muscles of the neck and shoulders, which soon become callous and give no pain.

A three-mile gait of the polemen moves the boat at each set a little more than its length, which gives, in ordinary water, a speed of over three miles an hour.

It requires as much skill and tact to handle the pole and get all there is in it of force as a propeller, as to use the oar. Notice how the men set and handle their poles—those on the left side of the boat grasp theirs with their right hand just below the button (the socket being in the water), and with a twist of the wrist and the help of the right knee the pole is thrown into the right position. The button is then brought to the shoulder and the force applied. This is done so quick and deftly that it seems like one motion. Upon reaching the stern of the walking board the poleman quickly rises, gives the pole a twist to disengage it from the bottom, and at the same time turns and grasps it with his left hand, walks to the bow and sets again. They must all set together and at the same time. The disengaged hand is always ready to grasp anything in its reach, either to increase the force of the push, or save oneself from going overboard if the pole should slip on the bottom. The skill and judgment of the steersman keep the boat parallel with the stream, and avoid a sideway motion; that would crowd the poles on one side, and be too far off on the other. When this happens the men break their hold and have to set again, which causes confusion.

While the crew are forwarding the boat, let us look at our surroundings. The sloping banks on either side, extending to higher land beyond, divided into alternate strips (woods and

THE ARNDT HOMESTEAD

The oldest house in De Pere. Built about 1836–37

cultivated land), and the French claims granted to the first settlers some years ago by the right of occupation. They are from two to five or six acres wide and extend back from the river eighty acres or more. Their owners have cleared and cultivated just enough to supply their present wants, leaving the original forest on [illegible]. All that each Frenchman wanted was a narrow strip of land on the river front where he could catch his fish (which he called his pork barrel), and the forest behind for wood and timber. On his cleared land he raises potatoes, wheat, oats, and other grain, while with gun and rod he supplies the rest of his provender whether of fish, flesh, or fowl.

That house which we are passing, a few rods from the river shore, is the residence of Jourdain, a blacksmith, whose shop is just north of the house. He is an old settler and a very worthy one, father-in-law of the Rev. Eleazer Williams.

Next comes John Lawe's point. The platform there erected is used to dry lyed corn, which is the food of his employees. He is one of the old settlers, one of the few influential men of this region. You can see from his dwelling, garden, parks, and outhouses how he lives in patriarchal style like the old Dutchmen on the Hudson River, a hundred and fifty years or more ago.

Here is another point, called that of Louis Grignon, on which is an old storehouse. Forty or nfty rods east, on an elevation, is his dwelling, an old house in the style of buildings built about seventy or eighty years before. He, too, is an old settler, born here and belonging to one of the oldest families. A few rods south of this dwelling, and close to the south line of the farm, is the schoolhouse—on Louis Rouse's farm, whose house is a few rods south. I went to school here for a short time, the teacher being Captain Curtis, afterwards succeeded by A. G. Ellis.[5]

The bank here takes a sudden rise, forming a steep descent from the road above to the water's edge, and covered with a heavy growth of trees and underbrush. This continues some distance up the river, where it descends to a low but narrow

---

[5] For documents on early schools at Green Bay, see *Id*, xii, pp. 453–465; see also Ellis's "Recollections," *Id*, vii, pp. 228–231, 234–236.—Ed.

table-land, breaking the monotony of the view and lending beauty to the scene.

Observe a house on that low bank near the river's shore. There once lived a man, owner of the neighboring farm, named Beauprey.[6] He was a trader in the olden time and died a singular death from the excessive use of green tea. He became so fond of it that he drank it night and day, and even ate the grounds. Of this excess he died, and singular to tell, his complexion changed to a deep tea-green.

The river is now widening. We are entering the suburbs of what is known as "Shanty Town." This settlement is due to a mistake on the part of a United States officer in locating the troops in the wrong place—Camp Smith. A mile or more away, to the southeast, on that higher elevation, two or three buildings still remain of the old camp. This camp started the boom of "Shanty Town," which is built on the west side of the second plateau near its brink—the shanties are of one story with a basement; all kinds of material were used in their construction, and no particular style of architecture. However, they answered the purpose for which they were built, and when no longer of use were left to time and decay. Daniel Whitney, the Irwins, and William Dickinson had built better, substantial, comfortable dwellings and stores. The glory of this inland city has gone into history. It was doomed when the order came to move the soldiers from Camp Smith.[7]

Push on. The scene is about the same, although the forest is more dense and approaches nearer to the water's edge. The river is fast widening. We are approaching the site of the oldest mission in the Northwest. The Jesuit mission of Rapides des Pères was established by Father Claude Allouez in 1669. Three or four small modern buildings mark the place where that heroic priest preached the gospel to the benighted Indians.

A new and bolder scene now presents itself. Higher and more abrupt banks reach the margin of the river, covered with a heavier growth of forest trees, dipping their pendent limbs in the fast-flowing stream. The stream is not as straight as it was below; the jutting points are more prominent and look as

---

[6] For a sketch of this person see *Id*, xix, p. 364, note 10.—ED.

[7] For this episode see *Id*, xx, and references therein cited.—ED.

though they barred the way. We turn the point, and other headlands appear, each with a beauty of its own.

The current now grows stronger; the Little Kaukauna is near. That long, narrow, low-lying island which you see to the right, is the home of the Rev. Eleazer Williams. He has a considerable tract of land west of his dwelling, given to him by the Oneida Indians, who were located here a few years ago. Here are the rapids known as Little Kaukauna, sometimes very difficult to pass. If the river is high we can push through that short canal to the right, which was a flume or waste weir. At an early date the United States built a mill here, but owing to a faulty construction of the dam, which soon gave way, it was abandoned.[8] As the river is about at the right stage, a few quick and vigorous shoves of the poles will soon take us through that quick-running mass of troubled water.

Well done, my good and gallant crew! The halfway stake is passed, and not half the day gone. Moor the boat and rest a spell while we lunch and refresh the inner man. The time is up and we proceed. The only change in the general landscape is the receding of the high bank from the river, leaving along the shore long narrow strips of low land. The same dense forest crowds to the water's edge.

Note those hieroglyphics on the oak trees that stand leaning over the water. They are made to represent a deer, and sometimes the hunter in the act of firing his gun. They record the hunter's success in the chase. There are hundreds of them all along the shores, many of them well executed and painted with vermillion. In June, when the deer are in the red, and seek the water, the Indian places a torch in the bow of his canoe with a screen behind which he hides gun in hand ready to shoot, while his companion slowly and noiselessly poles and manages the canoe. The deer is an inquisitive animal; the light attracts his attention, he approaches and falls an easy victim to the cunning of the hunter.

Here is Apple Creek, a small stream putting in from the west; the high bank on the east side is receding from the shore, showing a widening strip of low and level land. Then comes Plum Creek, quite a large stream; and there is the second house

---

[8] See *Id*, vii, p. 229.—Ed.

that we have seen since we left De Pere. It is occupied by Hoel S. Wright, a shrewd Yankee who keeps a store and trades with the Indians for furs and will put up any belated traveler who happens along.

Among the Rapids

We are now approaching Rapides des Croches, a difficult place to pass. Here at this short turn of the river, the water runs swift and deep over a bottom of smooth rock and large boulders, some of whose tops come near the surface and are not easily avoided. This makes the poling bad, since the poles slip on the smooth rock and the poleman is liable to be thrown overboard.

This place has a history. It was neutral ground between two hostile tribes, the Winnebago and Menominee. Here in times past they met and tried to settle their differences and to trade. The Winnebago had wild rice to exchange. This grew in great abundance along the lakes and rivers in their possession. The Menominee built bark canoes and were willing to barter these for rice and other things. The Winnebago craft were nothing but clumsy and ill-built dug-outs that did not properly serve them for the gathering of rice and fish on their large lakes, and travelling on their many rivers. The Winnebago desired to possess canoes, and I suspect that the Menominee always got the best of the bargain.

From here to the Grignon landing, the poling is much easier than below, since the current is less swift. As we ascend, the banks on either side are increasing in height. The forest still dominates the scene, and is densest on the eastern slope.

The Great Kaukauna

We are now approaching a panoramic scene of high lands clothed in primitive forest, sweeping around from north to south, then toward the western heights, then north to opposite the starting point on the eastern bank—making a circuit of seven or eight miles and enclosing one of the most beautiful and picturesque scenes on the lower Fox. Through this region of glades and meadows, gentle slopes or abrupt ascents, the river comes rolling and tumbling along from the westward over and around the great rocks, fretting and foaming as though in anger at the obstructions [illegible] but at last it turns to the north in quiet and peace [illegible] in which in the proper season thousands of fish appear—in numbers almost equalling the leaves on the forest trees. The strong rapids above barring their way, they crowd in [illegible] that the spearsmen seldom miss their aim; [illegible] name Kaukauna, which means enough, plenty.[9]

This part of the valley is owned in partnership by Augustin Grignon and John Lawe. The first or lower landing belongs to the former; the upper, about one and one-half miles higher, to Lawe. That cluster of buildings about a mile away northwestward sheltered by the hills, is Augustin Grignon's residence. His dwelling, outhouses, store, barns, and stables are in the olden style, and his farm is cultivated and managed in the primitive mode of the last century. Born and raised at Green Bay, he has spent all his life in the Indian trade, and in later years this has been his principal trading post. He has a beautiful place and the part he uses for the farm is under a good state of cultivation, notwithstanding the old style.

Here our agent has everything in readiness for tomorrow's portage; the men and teams will be on hand by daylight. Notice the men unloading the boat. Goods liable to be injured by rain are put in a pile by themselves and covered with oil cloths. Those not requiring such protection are placed in another pile, so that they can be hauled first by the teams and stowed in the bottom of the boat, and the other goods placed on top to keep them dry in case some accident should happen among the rocks and the boat spring a leak. In such an emergency we beach the boat, unload, and repair damages.

An Indian Village

The men have unloaded the boat, protected the piles of freight from rain, and pitched the tents. Supper is eaten before the sun goes down, and then we smoke a pipe and gaze at the beautiful scene surrounding us. Look to the east, a mile away over the moving water. See that sloping hill extending a mile

---

[9] Usually interpreted as "a fishing ground for pickerel."—Ed.

or so along the shore, reached at an easy angle from the beach. A distance of more than a thousand feet has been terraced and forms a succession of broad plateaus on which the Indians have built in irregular lines their huts and wigwams, utilizing every available space for the cultivation of corn, potatoes, and other vegetables. It is a typical Indian village, with its terraced farms extending in long lines along the slope, dotted at irregular intervals with their quaint and picturesque dwellings.

Let us now retire to our tent and sleep, for we have before us the greatest obstacle of the whole trip to overcome—rapids of fifteen miles, with very little slack water between.

When we reach Lake Winnebago we will be a hundred and forty or a hundred and fifty feet above the level of our present night camp. This is to be overcome by the skill, brawn, and muscle of about thirty men, wading and dragging the boat by main force against a strong current that will continue most of the way. The extra men are to be obtained from that Indian village on the slope beyond. This has been their business ever since Fox River boating commenced; they have learned the method and many of them are good pilots who can take command of the boat and push her through.

Here is the dawn of another day. The cook is preparing the morning meal, the Indians are launching their canoes to cross the river, and I can hear the squeak of home-made carts as they are driven down the road from Grignon's farm. In these primitive vehicles no iron is used save the tire, and often not even that; they surely need no horn to signal their approach.

The men are preparing the boat for a start, and the teams are loading. I leave one trusty man here with the agent, who will check the goods on to the wagons and when loaded follow them to the upper landing, and then return to check and unload again. Another man cares for the remaining goods. I also send another along with the teams to guard the goods when delivered at the upper landing where they are reloaded on to the boat.

The tents are struck and put on the boat for fear we may not reach the Grand Chute before night. In that case we will have to camp, for we can not run the rapids after dark. It is but eight miles from Kaukauna to the Grand Chute. If we have an hour and a half or two hours of daylight after arriving at the latter, we can unload and run the boat back to Kaukauna tonight. That depends on how soon the teams will haul enough freight to load the boat to suit the present stage of water. A half hour's delay here may make a difference of nearly a day in the rapids. I have directed the agent to hurry up the teams.

The boat and crew are now ready for a start. That tall, fine-looking Indian at the bow is Blacksmith[10], my pilot, and he is one of the best on the river. His only fault is that like the rest of the race, he is too fond of whiskey.

Notice how the water has here spread out, forming a small, shallow lake; but on the other side in the bight, or bend of the bay, it is much deeper. The roar of the waters as they rush down the rapids is much louder. You will soon see, as well as hear, the turmoil as they plunge down an incline of nearly forty feet in a little more than a mile.

Now comes the struggle of man with the physical forces of nature. The steering oar is unshipped; the mast is lashed across the boat to one of the beams, ten or twelve feet from the bow; the tow-line is made fast on one side, the same distance from the bow, and coiled ready for use. The men now arrange themselves around the boat. The pilot is at the bow, with his arm around the projecting point of the stem, where he has a good purchase; there are two or three behind him on either side, to assist in changing the direction of the boat; two or more are placed at the mast, where it projects beyond the boat; the rest take their positions along the sides. They have a good hold on the inner side of the walking board, to lift, push, or hold on.

The water varies in depth from about two feet to four, and the rocky bottom is very uneven. Notice how the men cross with the boat from one side of the river to the other. They do not turn and point the bow straight for the other shore. The craft must be kept parallel with the trend or course of the stream. If in a very still current, with rocks protruding here and there,

---

[10] For this Indian, whose aboriginal name was Wistweaw, see *ante*; also *Wis. Hist. Colls.*, xi, pp. 399, 400. Mrs. Kinzie calls him "the most accomplished guide through the difficult passes of the river;" see her *Waubun, passim*.—Ed.

the boat should take a swing and the men lose control of it, it would either fill with water and capsize, or becoming a perfect wreck endanger the lives of the crew. The pole lashed across the bow is a great help in such cases; one man alone can do what it would take four or five to accomplish by other means.

Here the river runs north of east, and at the foot of the rapids makes a big turn to the north. We are going up on the north side of an island, formed by a small outlet on the south. The island is covered with timber, mostly red cedar.

The Stockbridge Mission

Here we are safe and sound, moored at the upper landing in a little pool or eddy formed by a wing-dam made by Augustin Grignon to run a grist-mill which for many years he used frequently. To the south you have a view of part of the Stockbridge settlement. On that interval of low-lying land between the river and the hill to the south, are several dwellings extending up and down the river for one or two miles. These belong to the Presbyterian Mission, of which the Rev. Mr. Miner has charge.[11] His dwelling, out-houses, and other necessary structures are about the centre of the tract. The situation is a pleasing one—the river in front, backed by the green hills and the towering forest, with intervening farms and dwellings.

The Stockbridges are both physically and intellectually a much finer race than the other New York Indians. They are more civilized, live more like the whites, and show less of the Indian in their character and habits. Their dwellings are better built, their farms better cultivated, and all their surroundings show more brains, thrift, and enterprise. Their farms extend about four miles, from Kaukauna to the Cedars, well banked from the river, for the frontage of the stream is much broken in places; their land is well timbered and of heavy growth.

---

[11] For documents on the Stockbridge mission, see *Wis. Hist. Colls.*, xv, pp. 39 ff, including the papers of the Rev. Jesse Miner.—Ed.

Pioneers and Durham Boats on Fox River

Re-embarking

The teams have arrived with their loads—eight of them, which means between seven and eight tons. We will hurry and unload the wagons, and in about two hours be ready to start for the Grand Chute.

We soon take the stream, the water reaching to the knees and often to the waist, as it rushes foaming past. With a death-like grip the men cling to their hold, and step by step force the boat against the swift-running current. True to his instinct, the pilot motions with his hand the direction to take, straight ahead or to the right or left, always careful to keep the boat in line with the current.

We are now passing Daniel Whitney's potashery. This is one of the enterprises that he has carried on for a number of years in places where ashes could be obtained. When the Stockbridges located here he opened a store and building an ashery induced them to save all the ashes they made, either in their dwellings, or from log heaps they burned in clearing their farms. As the timber was very heavy and mostly of hard wood, a large quantity of the best ashes were obtained and converted into potash at a good profit to Mr. Whitney and to the great benefit of the Indians.

Here for more than a mile the river is deep and the current swift and strong. The banks are broken by gulches on either side. The higher land advancing and receding at short intervals, leaves but small strips of low or meadow land, so that the location on the river bank is not as desirable and pleasant here as below Kaukauna. For this reason the Indians have built their dwellings and opened their farms back from the river. It is only now and then you catch a sight of their homes, their clearings seldom reaching the stream.

The Little Chute, a little over three miles from Kaukauna, is not a difficult point to pass—the lift of the rock is only eighteen or twenty inches, and as the river widens some the flow is lessened. At the place we pass up, the rock has been cut away, to render it more easy to pass up or down.

We are now passing a low, open glade on our right, with a high bold bank to the left, which is called the Cedars. Why it is so called I cannot tell, for the timber is hard wood—white and black oak, of the finest growth, tall and straight.

The poling is good, although the current is strong but lessening as we progress, for the still water is near. When we pass that bold jutting point to the right we will enter a placid stream, languidly moving along as if fatigued with its struggle over the rocks above and forgetful of the obstructions below. The change is sudden from the noise and turmoil of the water as it rushes among the rocks below, to the stillness of this gentle stream as it flows with scarce a ripple on its smooth surface. As we pass along up the stream we catch the echo of rushing water tumbling from obtruding rocks, low at first but louder as we advance, until the whole scene bursts upon us of a wide, mad river falling four feet over a perpendicular rock, and then rushing on for more than a mile over hidden and protruding rocks until it is lashed into foam.

The Grand Chute

We are now approaching the Grande Roche. We will put up our poles and take to the water. This is the most difficult place on the river to pass with a loaded boat. It is similar in its formation to the Croche, only on a larger scale; the river is contracted by the west bank, forming a point, while the east shore is almost straight. The banks are abrupt and high, and as you turn the point the river spreads out into a bay towards the west, making a great curve to the Grand Chute above. The current on the east side, flowing in nearly a straight line, meets the flow from the curved line and causes a cross current that piles up the water in great confusion and makes the passage difficult. With a smooth rock bottom and great boulders strewn about, many quite near the surface, with insufficient water above them to float the boat, it requires great care to guide the craft in safety through this turmoil. As the water is deep, often reaching to the armpits, it paralyzes half the strength of the men; their only safety is to cling to the boat and inch by inch force her through the flood.

The roar of the Chute above, mingling with the noise of the fast-flowing rapids below and around, tries the strength and courage of the hardy boatmen, but they are equal to the task.

With a whoop and a rush they enter the troubled water and breast the fearful tide; the victory is soon won, the haven is near.

From here you get a front view of the whole scene—the Grand Chute, about a mile away, pouring its water over a rocky ledge. As it strikes the inclined ledge below it is beaten into a sea of foam, which like flakes of snow is carried down the stream at railroad speed. The banks around the bay are high, bold, abrupt, reaching to the water's edge, covered as usual with a heavy and thrifty growth of timber. From this camping ground a trail leads to another above the Chute, over which portages were made by the earlier navigators; it leads over the hills to the right, a long and tedious walk, but there is no other path, for the bluffs along the river shore bar the way.

Let us pass on and up, for our time is short, and we have much hard work to do before we reach our goal. We must take to the water again, for poles are useless against the strong current, and numerous protruding rocks strew the way.

To the right, where the ledge starts from that high, steep bank, is the point where we land and unload. You can see the ladders laid along the shore close under the bluff, supported on stone, to raise them above the shallow water. These ladders extend a short distance above the Chute to a landing that has been dug out of the bluff, forming a platform large enough to store the goods and pitch a tent in case of need. On this side, also, we will pass the boat over the Chute, as there is a greater flow of water here than on the other side. We now unload the boat and leave two or three men to move the freight to the upper landing and look to its safety.

The boat now being lightened, away she goes down the stream, with the swiftness of the wind. Notice how the pilot steers the boat, straight for that big boulder that seems to approach us so rapidly. As the boat nears the rock the bow is raised by the piling up of the water above it, and she gracefully glides to one side as if making her obeisance to the passing rock, the pilot at the same time moving the stern in the same direction, which brings the boat parallel with the current. Thus on we go at race-horse speed from rock to rock, the shores, banks, and trees gliding past, while it seems as if we alone stood still.

We are now approaching the still water, and will use the

oars again. The crew, to relieve the tedium of the slow passage down this stretch of dull water, give us a lively French boatman's song. They use a short, quick stroke and beat the time with their oars. The leader first sings a line of the song and repeats it; then the chorus is sung by the whole crew with a force and strength that makes the welkin ring as the echoes roll back from shore to shore.

Lay by the oars, for the rapids are near. The ripple of fast-flowing water is around us, the rocks seem again to be going up the stream, the forest flying swiftly by. We are now passing the Cedars; how quickly and smoothly we glide along!

We near the Little Chute, whose roaring we now can hear. See the foaming crest as the water plunges over the ledge. Through it we rush so quickly that ere we realize where we are the Chute is past and far astern, the crew shouting with all their might at the successful plunge we made. On we speed like a bird on the wing; the ashery is past and we hear the rumbling of Kaukauna Rapids below. Our landing is reached, and the boat rounded to with the bow up stream, ready for her second load.

Thus one day's work in the rapids is completed. We are not always so successful, but everything has been in our favor—the water at a good stage, the day long and the weather fine, with no rain to hinder us. Besides, I had the pick of the extra men, for there is no other boat in the rapids. Very low or very high water, short days, rain, and several boats on the river at the same time, combine to lengthen the time of transit and of course to increase the cost.

You and I, my reader, will not ride up on the boat to-morrow, but walk. As soon as she leaves the landing we will start, for it is only eight or nine miles on a good trail, and this will take us about three hours. You can see the lay of the land and enjoy the beautiful scenery along the banks and admire the splendid forest trees that crown the land. I will take my gun along, for we may get a partridge or two, or some other game.

We should be able to get the boat over the Grand Chute, load her and go into camp at the Grand Encampment before dark, and to-morrow reach Big Butte des Morts. We are now about half way to the Chute from Kaukauna; this is a much travelled trail and has been used for hundreds of years by the natives of the region. See how deep the path is worn by the travel of the light-stepping savages.

Here is the lower Grand Encampment, where we were yesterday, in full view of and below the Chute. The trail turns here to the right and follows around the bay over some deep gullies. There comes the boat, just through the Grande Roche. See them breast the stream, each man doing his best, for they know that this is the last long pull to reach the Chute, and their day's work is nearly done.

To unload the boat and pull her over the Chute is a short job with the number of men and the appliances we have. While the crew are unloading, the extra men will move the balance of the freight to the upper landing. We will then be ready to pass the boat over the Chute. The purchase we use is two strong blocks, with a suitable line. The first block is hooked into the ring of the eyebolt in the stem of the boat, and the tackle is fleeted; the other block is made fast to that large tree above the Chute, which is in line with the pull. A snatch-block is also used, through which the fall is led that enables the men to stand on the shore, which gives them a better chance to pull, besides increasing the power of the purchase. Some of the rock has, for quite a space, been removed from the top of the ledge, forming an inclined plane, which increases the flow at that point, lessens the lift, and renders it much easier to ascend.

The boat is now moved out to the place of ascent, the purchase is hooked on, and we are ready. As the strain on the purchase increases, the men at the bow of the boat lift all their might. At first she moves slowly, but when she strikes the broader part of her bottom it aids the men to lift, and the blocks and tackle do the rest. Hand-over-hand, with shouts that almost drown the roar of the Chute, this noisy crew land the boat at the upper landing, which is a couple of boat-lengths above the brink of the falls.

Grand Encampment

The worst obstacle has been met and overcome. The rest of the journey is in comparison, but play. We have time to reach the upper Grand Encampment before dark. This is an old trading post, owned by Charles Grignon, situated on a low piece of land and a mile or so above the Chute, where the early voyagers packed their goods in passing up or down the rapids. A road is now being made from Kaukauna to this point, to save the wear and tear of the boats and also to lessen the expense in money and time.

The scenery along the shores is changing. We are leaving the higher lands behind and entering a lower range of country; the flow of the stream is slow and gradually expanding; the timber is not so fine, being of a more scrubby growth than below. We will rest here on this old camp ground in peace and quiet for the night, and not trouble ourselves with the cares of to-morrow.

Breakfast being stowed away next morning, the tent is struck, the mast put in place, and we hoist the canvas and sail away over the bright water of this glorious river. We do not often have such a chance as this; but we always take it when it comes, for the poling through this stretch of the river to Lake Butte des Morts is difficult on account of the muddy, oozy bed of the stream. The poles are laid aside, and the oars are now useless; the sail is up, the boat is on the wing, and apparently by her own volition she plows a broad furrow through the limpid waters.

Little Butte des Morts

We are now entering Little Butte des Morts Lake—so named from a mound or Indian burying ground, the site of the Indian treaty of 1827. The beautiful lake, with a varied conformation of high and low lands, sweeps around in a grand circuit of several miles. On the east side, where the curve begins, are two inlets flowing from Lake Winnebago, forming a large island called Four Legs, the name of one of the principal Winnebago chiefs, who has a considerable village on the eastern end of the island.[12] These inlets are the Winnebago Rapids. The east side of the lake, as well as the island, is covered with a fine dense growth of timber of various kinds, while at the west and south, around the head of the lake, the timber is sparse and prairie land begins.

[12] For this chief see Powell's "Recollections," *ante*.—Ed.

Pioneers and Durham Boats on Fox River

Winnebago Rapids

Here we are at the foot of the Winnebago Rapids. Take in the sails and man the poles. The place where we stop to unload a part of our cargo is an old camp-ground, a short distance above this to the left, on Four Legs Island. I will send a man above to measure the water at the shoalest place, so that I can load the boat to suit the depth, for the depth of water she draws is marked on stem and stern. These rapids are not difficult to pass, save for the shallow places and the trouble of unloading and loading and making the two trips. This is the western branch of the rapids, where there is more water and fewer boulders than in the eastern. We will use the poles and not have to wade, unless we ground the boat on some of the shoal places; then we will have to take to the water to get her off. The water is reported at a fair stage. I will take the larger half of the load this time, choosing the lighter articles and those that will be loaded on top when we reload.

The place where we will load our boat for the last time on the lower Fox, is a point formed by Lake Winnebago on one side and a curve or bend of the river on the other, making a little cove or bay, safe from the wind. It is, and has been from olden time, a favorite camping ground of the Indians and *voyageurs* in this region—a beautiful place, with banks of moderate height covered with verdant grass, crowned by a growth of grand old trees that have given shade and shelter to the aborigines for hundreds of years. This is the point where the hardy boatman abides his time to cross the lake—a harbor of refuge from storms that at times sweep over its water.

Lake Winnebago

Here we are in good time at this beautiful camping ground. Lake Winnebago is surrounded on the north and east by a dense forest, mostly of various kinds of hard wood. Beginning at the eastern outlet, the shores gradually rise until you reach the eastern side, where the banks become bluffs on a base of limestone of considerable height. This formation continues for several miles up the lake. Then the high lands begin to recede from the shore, and the low lands gradually widen and expand into broad prairies at the head of the lake, and on the west side as far up as the Big Butte des Morts; they extend also many miles to the south.

On the east end of Four Legs Island, you can see his village of huts, built of bark supported on poles. Some of the lodges are twenty feet long, ten feet wide, and seven or eight feet high, rounded at the top with a space for the smoke to escape. This is his summer camp; here he gathers his wild rice, plants his corn and vegetables, dries his fish, and hunts his summer game.

Four Legs is one of the principal Winnebago chiefs, and influential with his people. I first saw him in 1826, when he passed through Green Bay on his way to Drummond Island, where the British had a garrison and distributed presents to the various tribes that had been loyal to them. He was then accompanied by a suite of ten or twelve men and two or three women, and escorted by his son-in-law, a white man named Gleason, as far as Green Bay. This man Gleason[13] was a singular genius; undoubtedly he was a Yankee by birth, shrewd, cunning, always looking out for number one. He had established a trading post on the east side of Lake Puckaway, and did a fair amount of trade through the influence of his Indian father-in-law. His wife was neither comely nor interesting, either in figure, face, or motion; her walk was like that of a sailor, and their two children had the same peculiarity. Gleason explained it in this way: when he built his house, no sawed lumber was to be had for the floor, so he split the logs in halves, stripped the bark, and laid the round side up, which corrugated the floor. His wife and children walking over these puncheons, gave this peculiar motion to their gait. I have often been in the house, for our boats generally had something for Gleason in the shape of goods or provisions. He was one of father's customers, being supplied by him with goods, for which he gave furs in return—mostly coon skins and badger, these being scarce in our part of the territory.

When Four Legs returned from Drummond Island, he was fitted out with a scarlet coat adorned with gilt buttons and

---

[13] For Luther Gleason, said to be from Vermont, see *Wis. Hist. Colls.*, vii, *passim;* also *Waubun*, pp. 54, 56, 350.—Ed.

O'-CHECK-KA, OR FOUR-LEGS

Winnebago chief, as he appeared at the Treaty of Green Bay, 1827
From colored lithograph by James Otto Lewis

lace, and was topped by a much ornamented cocked hat. Gleason, who came down while he was at the Bay, advised father to give the chief a suit and dinner, which he did. A sumptuous feast was prepared and set forth in an outhouse, and the chief and his companions enjoyed it without stint. Gleason was toast-master and dispensed the tea (the only beverage) with a princely hand befitting the son-in-law of the head-chief of a free and independent nation.

All aboard for Big Butte des Morts. To get good poling, we shall have to follow the meanderings of the various bays, which lengthens the distance, but the wind is off shore and this gives us smooth water.

How smoothly and easily the boat with her load of thirty tons moves along under the force of the poles. She makes about ninety feet at each set and rise, which will give us over thirty miles a day. It is about 130 miles from Big Butte des Morts to Fort Winnebago, but we will make it easily in four days, weather permitting.

Garlic Island marks about ten miles from the head of Winnebago Rapids; Big Butte des Morts, where we will camp, is four miles farther. This island cut quite a figure in the War of 1812, being the headquarters of Col. Robert Dickson, British agent and superintendent of the Western tribes.[14] It is a beautiful island, a few rods only from the mainland, round in form, with a small crescent-shaped bay on the land side. There are no large trees upon it, but a thrifty growth of young saplings as thick as they can grow, surrounding a cleared space of about an acre in the centre, forming a complete windbreak and shelter from every storm. It is the completest camp-ground I ever stepped on. There is a heavy growth of long tangled grass, as soft and yielding as a feather bed. I wish I might avail myself of it tonight, but we must leave this paradise of camps and push on to Big Butte des Morts.

---

[14] William Powell, in his "Recollections", *ante*, p. 151, states that Dickson's headquarters, the winter of 1813-14, were on the neighboring mainland. But Arndt's memory appears to be confirmed by the fact that in *Wis. Hist. Colls.*, xi, p. 278, is a letter by Dickson, dated specifically "Garlic Island"; although others of his many letters during the winter, in the same volume, are dated merely "Winebagoe Lake" or "Lac Puant".—Ed.

Here is our camp-ground; pitch the tent, prepare and eat our evening meal, and rest until the morning star warns us of the near approach of another day.

Big Butte des Morts

Big Butte des Morts was once the site of an old Indian village. The land is high and covered with a fine growth of timber, with intervals of open grassy glades. The lake is of considerable extent, with its receding bays and jutting points, dotted here and there with islands of various forms, adding much to the beauty of the scene.

As we pass along to where the upper Fox enters this lake, I will explain our commissary department. Our staple provisions consist of salt pork, flour, beans, wild rice, tea, and sugar, supplemented by game, fish, or fowl that we gather along our way. The men all know how to cook this simple fare; the best one is chosen, however, and the others assist. The cooking is mostly done at night, soup being the favorite dish, made with wild rice or beans, pork, and other meat. The meat is put into a large camp-kettle with sufficient water, and at the right time the rice or beans which have been soaked during the day, are put in and boiled all night with a slow fire, so as not to burn or scorch. It will be ready for our breakfast and also for dinner; for supper, the meat and potatoes (if we have any) will be fried. We have tea at every meal, plenty of it, hot and well sweetened. This saves time, for all we have to do when we stop for breakfast or dinner is to boil the water for this beverage.

We always travel an hour or two before breakfast, which gives us a good appetite and the soup is then just at the right temperature. We often vary this when we get a fat deer, by roasting a part of it during the night to supplement our breakfast and dinner. For our bread, we mix flour and water to the right consistency, with salt and a little saleratus; the dough is then put into a large frying pan and turned frequently until it is hard enough to stand on its edge without bending or breaking. It is then placed on edge around the fire, supported by a board or a couple of sticks, near enough to brown it nicely and not burn; the change from side to side is frequently made, to insure success and bake it through and through. All of this cooking is done neatly and with dispatch; and all the utensils used are washed, wiped, and put away in a large mess chest, ready for use after each meal.

The Upper Fox

If my reader will steer the boat for a little while, I will take the extra pole and see if another man increases the speed. Hold on, you have missed the Fox, you are going up the Wolf; you should have turned to the left. That narrow opening through the weeds and grass is the upper Fox. This is a custom established by the early navigators of the river. When the boat or canoe arrives at this point, the stranger is asked to steer. If he misses the upper Fox, and takes to the Wolf, as you have done, he pays a small forfeit to the crew. This generally is a bottle or so of wine or whiskey, deliverable on our arrival at Fort Winnebago.

Now starboard your helm and run her through that narrow gap, and we will soon see the upper Fox. The scenery at and near this entrance of the river to Lake Butte des Morts would be tame and uninteresting if it were not for the grand sweep of prairie land, seen through vistas of timberland on the east; while on the west side it is low and swampy, backed by high timbered land in the distance. The current of the river is slow, there being but thirty feet of fall from the Portage to this place, about 125 miles. It is supposed to be as crooked a navigable river as ever was made. The Indian legend of its formation is something like this:

An Indian Myth[15]

Long, long ago, soon after the beginning of things, a monstrous serpent, wise and cunning, lived in the Mississippi River. He became dissatisfied with his home and desired to visit the Great Lakes. So one day in the early spring he started on his journey. He first ascended Wisconsin River, making a great noise and commotion, throwing up sand banks and making

[15] See allusion to this myth in *Waubun*, pp. 56, 57.—Ed.

shallow places, completely changing the natural flow of the river which before this had been a beautiful running stream without obstructions. When he arrived at the Portage the water from the Wisconsin was flowing over it, in a northerly direction. The ground over which the water flowed from the Wisconsin was low and swampy, being nearly level; the water was shallow and ran very slow and spread over a large tract of country. He made his way over and through this shallow water until he struck a small stream flowing north. He plunged in and soon widened and deepened its narrow channel to accommodate his huge body and gather in the water flowing across the Portage and help him along on his journey. He worked and wormed along in many directions, seeking a better place to pass. At last, after many turns from north to south and from west to east he found the place that he thought would do. He soon cleared a space sufficiently large to suit him, and as the abundant game suited his taste he concluded to remain and enjoy himself as best he might. This place is now called Mud Lake.

He remained here during many moons, gorging himself with his favorite food, until he had consumed or driven away his supply. Hunger forced him to renew his journey. He now struck a different formation of sand, thrown up into ridges and hillocks, the drift of the glacial period. Of this he made short work, soon throwing out a long channel of considerable width and several miles in length which became a long narrow lake, called by the Indians Buffalo Lake, because the last buffalo ever seen in this part of the country was chased into it and drowned.

Here the serpent remained for some time. Buffalo and deer were plenty and he enjoyed himself right royally. The water increased and formed a large lake; a high bank, or moraine, formed a dam and held the water back. The noise and confusion he made caused the game to leave this region. Having nothing to eat, he concluded to continue his journey, broke through the opposing bank, and he and the water rushed on to the next resting place, which was but a short distance below, where another bank intervened and barred the way for a time. But exerting his tremendous strength he removed the obstruction and moved on, leaving still another lake, now called Puckaway, from its many reeds or rushes, of which the Indians make their mats. The land to the right, or east, being high and piled up in great ridges, he concluded to change his course to a more westerly one, for in this direction the way seemed more open. He therefore changed his tactics, and instead of going through the hillocks he went around them, steering his great carcass among these obstructions until he had boxed the compass many times.

He now came to a different country, where the obstructions were more formidable, land higher, rock and stone more compact and covered with a thick growth of forest. Nothing daunted, he rushed on, throwing his whole strength into the work. He scooped out a small lake which is now called Big Butte des Morts; by forming this lake he had tapped another supply of water to help him on his way, the Wolf River. Encouraged by this he moved along with more vigor and force to greater and more herculean deeds. Another lake of greater extent was formed; here he sported, rolled, dove, and swam to his heart's content. Being wise he knew by the peculiar glimmer at times in the eastern sky that his work was nearly done, that a large body of water lay off to the east and north, that the Great Lakes were near.

He made another circuit of the lake, now called Winnebago, to find the weakest part of the barrier. He chose the northwest portion, for there the land is lower; there he made the breach and scooped out a small lake below, called now Little Butte des Morts. After remaining there a short time, he concluded to visit Lake Winnebago again and enjoy himself. After a time the desire to reach the Great Lakes returned stronger than ever. When he returned to the outlet, Winnebago Rapids, he decided that he needed more water below to help him through the rocky stratum; so at it he went and soon accomplished the task.

On rushed, with its guide, the increased flood of water, tearing and rending the solid rock and removing the superincumbent earth and thus forming the Grand Chute. On went the work of reformation. The Little Chute was reached; the Grand Kaukauna was twisted and wrenched and the afterflow was left to complete the work, while the great tide swept on, left its mark at De Pere, and passed on wasting its strength in the Great Lakes. Subsequently the great fabulous serpent was swept over Niagara and perished ingloriously in its turbulent waters.

The Lakes of Fox River

We are moving along at our usual pace of a little over three miles an hour, gradually unwinding the crooks and turns of this serpentine river. To cheer and pass the time the bowsman as he breaks his set at the end of the push, and turns to walk to the bow, bursts forth into a merry song which breaks in echoes along the silent stream, each man marking time with his feet. In silence they reset their poles, push to the end, rise, and the whole crew break forth in a repetition of the line. Thus each line is sung to the end of the song.

Wearied of this, for a time a dead silence ensues, there being heard only the set of the poles and tramp of feet along the walking boards. Steadily they set, push, and rise, and the boat glides along over this smooth and gentle stream apparently with little effort. But here we are at our camping ground, nearly forty miles from the Butte.

Of the scenery I can say but little. It has a sameness not as pleasing as the lower Fox. Prairie and sparsely-timbered land, intermixed with the roll of the prairie on the east side, form in some places a grand spectacle. In a few places, where the river has made its way through the drift, there are bluffs of considerable height. We will try to reach Gleason's place on Lake Puckaway to-morrow, and another day and a half will put us at Fort Winnebago.

Just as the sun is rising, the boat is ready, and all are aboard. More twists and turns and points deviate our course, and within a few miles we have steered to every point of the compass. On the introduction of the larger and longer boats we were obliged to cut away many of these points, for there was not room to turn the bends. We always carry shovels and picks for this purpose, and to remove the sand-bars that form.

We will today pass an interesting point a few miles below Lake Puckaway—a hill of considerable elevation, at right angle with the river, forming a long narrow ridge, the north slope of which is an easy grade, the south side being steep. On the apex are two rows of mounds, each four of them forming a square of seventy-five or a hundred feet. The north row begins with a mound two or three feet high; to the east is another mound in exact line, a little larger than the first, and so on as far as I traced them, each succeeding mound increasing in size. The south row was in reverse order, diminishing in size going east, while the north row diminished running west, so that the four formed a square.

Lake Puckaway is in view from this point—long, narrow, and shallow, overgrown in part with reeds and rushes, hence its name. At Gleason's place on the east side we will make a short stop, and then go on to Buffalo Lake through a narrow channel that connects the two lakes. This is difficult to pass by reason of the shallow water and the crooks and turns, but we will reach the head of Buffalo Lake to-night and camp. This lake is long and narrow with high, irregular banks, mostly of sand, especially at the foot of the lake. Our camp is at last reached after a long, weary push. We are glad to rest and sleep.

The morning opens bright and clear. Push on, all together. Here is Mud Lake; well named, for there is nearly as much mud here as water. If the Fox is the crookedest river in Wisconsin, this lake has more mud to the square foot than all the other lakes in the Territory put together. Its bottom, if it has any, is far below the reach of our longest pole. We are obliged to use our oars to cross this reservoir of mud, until we can again find water and a bottom for our poles.

The Fox turns and twists around these points and bends. We face the north, then the east, the south, and the west, and back again. But we are making progress now; there is the fort, the bends unwind, the points grow less, the river straightens a few more shores and here is our landing. A small crowd greets us—the officers from the fort, the sutler, and a few settlers from the west side of the river. The arrival of a boat from Green Bay is quite an event for the residents of this place, who receive most of their supplies from our town.

Fort Winnebago

We will unload the boat and prepare for her passage down the river at the peep of dawn. Meanwhile the goods will be checked and the necessary papers made out, so that there need be no delay. In preparing the boat for her return trip, a fireplace will be built of stones and turf in the middle of the craft, in which to do our cooking. Other little arrangements will also be made for our comfort, so that there will be no let or hindrance in our passage down.

The Portage, or Fort Winnebago, is not a pleasant place as compared with many other locations on the Fox. The fort is built on a bluff on the east side, a short distance from the river fronting the south. The sutler's store is situated near the bank of the stream, not far from the fort. The shops and other necessary buildings are 1200 or 1500 feet south of the fort; the grounds, as is usual with army people, are kept neat and clean. A bridge connects the two sides, just below the sutler's store.

Just above the fort the river makes a turn to the east, along the higher land on that side, leaving on the west the greater part of the low lands, or portage. On a bluff about a half mile from the river, west of and nearly opposite the fort, are situated the Indian agency and the residences of some of the original settlers. This bluff sweeps around, trending to the west, until it strikes Wisconsin River about three miles southwest of the fort, forming a portaging place between the two rivers, Boats with their cargoes are portaged here on heavy wagons made for that purpose, and when launched on Wisconsin River make their way to Prairie du Chien or St. Louis.

When in 1829 the United States rebuilt Fort Winnebago,[16] contracts for building material were given out. Father took one to make and furnish all the brick, for he had all the implements used in brick-making, besides men skilled in the business. A year or two after the visit of Lafayette to the United States, father built a small-sized Durham boat which he named "Lafayette." She was a light, easy-running craft of from fifteen to twenty tons. This boat was loaded with brick-making tools and all necessaries, and with a crew of ten or twelve men

[16] The fort was built during the autumn of 1828; Arndt refers to the erection of additional and permanent buildings in 1829. See *Wis. Hist. Colls.*, xiv, pp. 65–74.—Ed.

was sent to Fort Winnebago. I went along as a sort of supernumerary.

It was in early June. The boat having a light load and a large crew ascended the rapids and in a few days reached Fort Winnebago. All arrangements for the work were soon made, and the place where the brick were to be made chosen—on the Wisconsin River about a mile and a half southwest of the fort. The work was well and quickly done under the superintendence of James Stewart from Ohio, whom father had employed for the purpose. The kiln could be seen for years thereafter.

Return Voyage

Early next morning we start on our downward way. The boat, being light, glides easily and swiftly along, and turns the points with ease. When we get through these short turns and have long reaches ahead, the wind being favorable, we shall make sail and push along faster. We should reach our camp of night before last by noon, and if the wind holds good, we may anticipate a fine sail through Mud and Buffalo lakes. This will continue down the outlet, most of the way into and through Lake Puckaway, until we enter the outlet or river where it takes a short turn to the west. There we will have to use our oars, unless the wind follows us around the bend.

We have been making good progress during the night, both with oars and sail. If this wind holds good, which I hope and think it will, there will be less rowing and poling and more sailing, and tonight we shall sleep at Winnebago Rapids. It is nearly noon, and the progress we are making will take us to Big Butte des Morts by the stroke of twelve. Here we are on this beautiful lake, with "a free sheet and a following wind." Let her go free in the open sea. She is moving lively now, for the wind is stronger here and increasing. We have passed the Butte and the high lands, and the low lands are on either side. When we make and turn that point to the right, Lake Winnebago will be seen.

The wind is stronger and more steady since we left the high lands and the shelter of the forest. We will keep the boat well out in the lake, to catch all the wind there is, and have a freer sheet, for the wind will follow somewhat the trend of the lake.

We are now on the open sea, with a fair wind. The boat is moving along like a thing of life, throwing the water from her sides as she swiftly passes through it. The day is waning, but we have time yet to reach our camp if this wind holds, for there is Garlic Island to the left and abreast of us. We are measuring off the miles at a great rate. See how quickly we reach from point to point; the last one, forming the outlet to the lake, and where we will camp, looms up and is growing nearer and more distinct every moment. Now we open the passage, and see the shores on either side. Starboard your helm, let go and haul the starboard sheet, luff. The boat turns the point and is safely moored for the night.

Arise my brave crew; one more effort on the home stretch and we will be there 'ere the sun sets. Cast off the lines, man the poles, give her to the current as it flows, and guide her straight from rock to rock. That was well done. These rapids are past, and here is Little Lake Butte des Morts. The wind is fair, hoist the sail and let her go.

Here is the Grand Encampment. Take in the sail and lower the mast, for we cannot jump the Chute and rapids with it standing; it might give us some trouble. Make everything ready and take the poles; we will push her down to the Chute, jump it, and let the swift-running water do the rest, except to guide and keep the boat parallel with the current.

Here she goes. The current has got the boat within its grasp; she is driven ahead on nearly a level keel more than a third her length before the bow dips to the incline below and makes the plunge. It is done so quickly and her motion is so rapid that you can hardly realize what has taken place before you find yourself a mile below the Chute and still going on at a railroad speed. If well done, it is grand and exciting and attended with but little danger.

We pass down, until we come to Grignon's (or the upper) landing. A little below this we strike the main rapids. The river is here contracted by an island on the east or south side. It is said that there is a fall here of nearly forty feet in a little over a mile. In one place the boat makes three tremendous plunges in succession. As she shoots along on the crest of the wave, the bow rises as she goes; when the crest is about midship, up goes the stern and the bow plunges into the foaming water ahead, throwing the spray clear to the stern of the boat. Thus three times she rises and plunges through this tumult of water, each time increasing her speed, which is fearful to see. The last blow given to these troubled waters was more terrific than the first; it made the boat tremble from stem to stern, but she recovers and glides along to more tranquil water. Thus we pass the rapids of the Grand Kaukauna to the still water below, where we hoist the sail and pass on down to Green Bay.

The trip which I have here described was made in twelve days—nine days on the upward journey and three on the return, besides some night work, using the sail on the return journey whenever possible. The distance from Green Bay to Fort Winnebago is 160 miles, which gives us about eighteen miles a day on the upward trip, and fifty-four or fifty-five on the return, including the night work. The distance travelled on the round trip (320 miles) makes an average of nearly twenty-seven miles per day during the long days of June.

The Durham monopolizes Traffic

After its introduction, the Durham boat was in constant use on Fox River between Green Bay and Fort Winnebago, and was some times used on Wisconsin River as far as Prairie du Chien, and even to Galena. It drove the French batteaux almost entirely out of use, as it carried a larger load and required fewer men to handle it. From the year 1825 until the completion of the improvement of Fox River, it was the usual means of transportation on that river.

As the business increased, more boats were built and improved. The open uncovered space between forward and after decks was housed with a strong but light frame, covered with a double course of half-inch pine boards, securely nailed and painted, the sides enclosed with adjustable shutters of the same material, making a dry comfortable cabin for either freight or passengers. Still other changes and improvements were introduced. The larger boats when completed and fully equipped for use, cost about a thousand dollars. To save their wear and tear in the rapids, smaller ones were built, something like the batteaux but with more beam and lower sides, whose tonnage was about a third of the larger boats and their cost much less. They were used in the rapids between Grand Kaukauna and Grand Chute, and were found to save both time and money. One set of the Durhams was used between Green Bay and Kaukauna, and another set between the Grand Chute and Fort Winnebago. The small boats were used exclusively until the road was finished, when the greater part of the goods were hauled from Kaukauna to the Chute by teams. This lessened the time in the rapids and the cost of transportation.

Three lines of boats competed for the business, so the price of the work was lowered and the profits lessened. Father could stand this competition better than those who were new in the business. He built his own boats, and in every respect was better equipped in men and material from his long experience in their use. Several parties tried the experiment of building their own boats, but did not succeed very well, for their craft proved to be too heavy and logy, being badly built.

Daniel Whitney, who had purchased several boats from father, thought he could build them cheaper himself. He found and hired a man from somewhere on the Mississippi, who said he knew all there was to know about the Durham boat. He set him to work at his ashery at the Grand Kaukauna, and began to collect the material.

Lumber was plenty and easy to get, but the iron work was another thing, especially the spike. Good blacksmiths were scarce. Father had a shop and blacksmith helper and had the blacksmithing done for his own boats. Mr. Whitney applied to him to do the work and make the spikes and bolts. The new boat builder had whittled out a pattern of a spike, about four inches long and 3/8 of an inch wide, a perfect wedge with a head on. Father at once said: "Mr. Whitney, that boat will never go up Fox River; that shaped spike will split every plank and timber in which you attempt to drive it, or if you use a bit large enough to drive without splitting it will leave a leak; and besides it will not hold the planking in their place without clinching. Your man is no boat builder, no mechanic, and your boat will be a failure."

Mr. Whitney was somewhat set in his way, and no argument

could induce him to change the shape of the spikes, so they were made as ordered and the result was as predicted.

The following spring the boat was launched after much trouble and expense. Mr. Whitney was by this time convinced that the boat was a failure as far as navigating the rapids of the upper Fox; she was too heavy, for a third more lumber was used than was necessary. She drew six or eight inches more amidship than she did before or after, besides other defects in her construction. He concluded if she would not do for the rapids and upper Fox he would take her to Navarino and make a wood and lumber raft of her. He put a big crew aboard and started down the rapids. After much time and hard work they got the boat below the Croche, but stuck her fast about half way between the Croche and Wrightstown, where she remained several weeks before they attempted to move her again. The bad construction of the boat and the hard knocks she received in going over the Grand Kaukauna, started the calking from the seams and made her leak badly. In course of time they got her to the Bay, fixed her up, and sent her to Duck Creek for a load of wood. The next morning after being loaded, she again sank, and this was, if I recollect rightly, her last trip.

The introduction of the Durham boat was a novelty to the people residing on the Fox. They declared at first that it would be an impossibility to force that big boat with its great load up and through the rapids; it would take lots of men and weeks to make the trip to the Portage. Better use the French batteau, to which they had long been accustomed. At the first trial of the boat they were dissuaded of their hereditary belief by the ease with which she passed along with her great load, and by the power and control that each man had with the shoulder, where his whole muscular strength as well as his weight could be applied. The small hand-pole used on the French batteaux had brought into play only muscles of the arms. The change of opinion was sudden. The Durham moved more easily through the water, we were not so tired when the day's work was done, even though we had shoved the big boat with a load—three times greater than that of the batteaux, more than thirty miles each day after clearing the rapids. Even on the upper Fox, because of her peculiar build she moved more easily than the batteau.

The crews were mostly made up of men born in Canada, who at an early age had enlisted in the service of the American Fur Company for a term of from five to ten years where their wages were low, and their food corn and tallow, eked out with the products of the chase. After completing their term of service, many of these men remained in the Green Bay settlement, soon married either a squaw or a woman of mixed blood, and large families were the result. The boys, as they grew to manhood, followed the pursuit of their fathers, or entered the transportation business, and made up the crews.

Recently a Prairie du Chien paper noted the death of Alexander Gardapie, an old *voyageur,* ninety years of age. He was one of the members of my favorite crew. He had been born and raised on a farm on the west side of the Fox, north of and adjoining that now owned by Isaac Dickey. Note the age at which he died, indicating the vigorous hold he had on life. This is but a sample of that once efficient crew and the men who composed it. Many of them lived to four-score years and beyond.

The Supreme Court of Wisconsin Territory[1]

By Robert George Siebecker

The act of Congress establishing the territorial government of Wisconsin, in 1836, provided for a territorial court of three judges, to whom was committed the high function of forming the system of civil courts designed by the general government, and of executing judicial power for a people who had theretofore lived in the free and unregulated state of primitive times. Under this act the president of the United States appointed Charles Dunn of Illinois,[2] David Irvin of Virginia,[3] and William C. Frazier of Pennsylvania[4] to constitute this tribunal. On July 4, 1836, the territorial government officers subscribed the oath of office at Mineral Point. The judges of this court did likewise and thus took the first step to establish courts for the infant territory of Wisconsin. The court first met to hold a session at this place, Belmont, on December of the same year. The executive and legislative departments of the territorial government had theretofore located here and legislative activities had been begun in a session commencing October 25, 1836. At this first session of the court Chief-Justice Dunn and Associate-

[1] Address delivered by Mr. Justice Siebecker of the Supreme Court of the State of Wisconsin at the unveiling of the tablet erected by the Wisconsin Federation of Women's Clubs on October 7, 1912, on the site of the first territorial capitol of Wisconsin at Leslie (formerly Belmont) in Lafayette County.—ED.

[2] See estimate by Martin in *Wis. Hist. Colls.*, xi, p. 408.—ED.

[3] Sketched by Draper in *Id*, vi, p. 379; see also *Proceedings*, 1911, pp. 182–186.—ED.

[4] See *Wis. Hist. Colls.*, i, pp. 127-130.—ED.

Justice Irvin were present and participated in the formal organization of the court by appointing a clerk, administering the oath of office to Henry S. Baird as territorial attorney-general, and admitting a number of persons to practice before the court; but no litigated matter was presented. The court adjourned and designated Madison as the place where it would convene in July of the following year, and there all subsequent meetings of the court have been held. These are the few and simple annals that tell the beginnings of the judicial history of the people inhabiting the beautiful and expansive domain of our State.

Turning our view further backward to the remote beginnings of white settlement in this territory, there arises in our minds a picture of the condition of a primitive wilderness abounding in all the natural resources that are needed to supply the wants of an enlightened people, awaiting only the skillful hand of man to convert them to his beneficial use. The people who undertook this great task well knew that this could be accomplished only under a well regulated society through the orderly processes of civil government, which would protect life and person, and secure to everyone the fruits of their labors and the blessings of their homes. To aid in accomplishing this was the high function of the courts as a branch of civil government. The social conditions that then existed, practically imposed on the inhabitants the necessity of employing individual power to protect themselves in their personal and property affairs, since the situation only admitted of an imperfect administration of law among the few and widely separated inhabitants.

Prior to 1823, judicial transactions of a minor character were confined to the local courts, before justices of the peace, and obviously they were administered in an irregular and desultory manner under the prevailing crude and unorganized conditions. All civil and criminal matters of a graver nature were under the law tried in the supreme court of the territory at Detroit, Michigan. This necessarily compelled the people to forego a resort to the courts for the enforcement of legal rights, on account of the great distances and lack of highways, as well as the other hardships and cost of travel. In 1823, Congress removed these difficulties in part by providing for an additional judge for that part of Michigan Territory lying west of Lake

Michigan. James Duane Doty, then twenty-four years of age, was appointed to this office, and continued in this service until 1832, when he resigned and was succeeded by David Irvin, who remained in office until the organization of the Wisconsin territorial government in 1836.

Until 1827 the appointed places for holding this court were at Green Bay, Brown County, and at Prairie du Chien, Crawford County; but at that time a change was made from the latter place to Mineral Point, Iowa County. Little is specifically known of the conduct of judicial transactions during these years. The tradition is, that the court met the needs of the community in a practical way, under the peculiar exigencies and occasions of the time, though its procedure for enforcing its mandates as an instrumentality of justice and social order was characterized at times by novel and unusual methods. It may be problematical whether or not a regular and orderly procedure, appropriate to an old and established community, would have been suitable to an efficient enforcement of law under the conditions of those early days.

Transgressions against the security of life and limb were by force of circumstances dealt with in a summary way, in order to restrain offenders from violations of the peace and good order. Under these circumstances the power conferred by the Ordinance of 1787, to promulgate civil and criminal law, could not readily be executed, for an employment of orderly procedure in the customary ways was materially hampered and restricted by the prevailing primitive state of affairs. Nor were the territorial judges and officers supplied with means to promulgate and enforce a system of procedure such as prevailed in older states and which had been evolved under more favorable conditions.

It is manifest that this new court began its activities in an environment devoid of the influences that had shaped the law of more thickly-settled and well-governed communities. The rapid increase in population after 1830 in the mineral-producing region and in the organized counties where the public domain was open for sale and entry, brought about the need for an efficient local self government to protect the various interests growing out of new and flourishing enterprises. The territorial courts, which constituted the pioneer institutions in the judicial history of our State, were established to meet this demand. Though the period during which they flourished was but brief, their influence gave birth to a system of courts that has maintained and promoted the peace and prosperity of the people of our State to this day.

Progress in establishing a system of law and courts appropriate to the necessities of the times was much accelerated by a rapidly-growing population and its expanding commerce and industry. As the people learned to know the possibilities of their surroundings, they framed laws which sprang from their necessities and from their aspirations for and ideals of freedom and self-government. Since their industry, commerce, and husbandry were undeveloped and engrossed their attention, it is natural that they developed a sense of responsibility pertaining to individual affairs rather than those concerned with public interests. We should therefore expect that the courts would devote their labors to protecting the private rights and interests of the people. This is manifest from their records, which show that they were principally occupied in redressing wrongs and enforcing rights of this nature. The environment and life of the people worked for simplicity and practically in the affairs of life. The spirit of actuality was potent in the administration of the law and became infused into its fabric. It was effective in suppressing useless ceremonial and conventional practices which served no useful purpose. This spirit tended to the adoption of the customs and usages of the times as the best means for the enforcement of the moral rules on a level with the people's practical ethical sense.

The ideas and practices infused into our law by these early courts has continued to mould the jurisprudence of our State and made it receptive to such changes and improvements as the progress of the people has demanded. We cannot doubt that these conditions were influential in developing the ideas and sentiments which found expression in our State constitution and our system of law and courts. Among the effective causes creating these favorable conditions was the sentiment of a common purpose, which later became operative, to promote the good of the people as a whole. This is a powerful incentive to aid in the building of a system of jurisprudence promotive of the common good. It tends to prevent the adoption of partial and technical regulations, regardless of their fitness to serve individual and public interests, and serves to foster practical equality.

The part played by the early judges materially aided the conditions favorable to the enactment of good laws and promotive of the fortunes of our people. Inspired by their conception of natural justice, the people's enthusiasm for good government received expression by them in a liberal and practical administration of the law. That these influences were an effective agency, influencing their judicial action, is shown with remarkable clearness and force as we study the course of the events that resulted in the formation of the people's institutions and laws. It promoted the spirit for improvement in legal procedure, culminated in the adoption of our code at an early day in the history of our State, and led to many reforms which simplified the law and accommodated it to the actual needs for a practical regulation of affairs, thereby developing among the people a respect for law which has been most potent in inspiring faith in their government as an agency under which they might secure the blessings of liberty and enjoy the fruits of their toil.

I rejoice that the power of this influence is not spent and that it operates today among our people to maintain a respect for government and to check the disdain for law and order which breeds the spirit that incites men to destroy their most beneficent institutions. It helps to keep before us the ideal of a system of laws which will further our best interests and protect us in the things we cherish as most sacred in life.

The achievements of our pioneer courts are an assurance that the judges composing them were men of probity and intelligence and of original and constructive thought. Of the three original appointees, Judge Frazier died October 18, 1838. It is said of him: "His career in Wisconsin was so brief and unimportant that but little is now remembered of it beyond the anecdotes found in the published *Collections* of the Wisconsin Historical Society, except that which is in a great degree traditional." Andrew G. Miller of Pennsylvania was appointed his successor.[5] As so constituted, these appointees held office until the organization of the State government in 1848. The history of their

[5] For a biographical sketch see *Id*, vii, p. 463.—Ed.

services shows that they were men of high judicial integrity and that they were impelled by an earnest fidelity and zeal to administer exact and equal justice. Their strong natural abilities and large capacities had been improved by training and culture. They fitted well into a generation in the legal profession when men stood on the solid ground of their individual power, and they were characterized by resolution and forcefulness. In their knowledge of men and things they were broad, and they dealt considerately with every class of the people in all their varying relations and interests. A knowledge of the wide range of affairs and conditions of their day, coupled with their professional learning, enlarged their views of life and cultivated in them the sagacity of men of the world. They stood in high esteem with members of the legal profession and the people, for their social virtues and for their devotion to a faithful discharge of their high official duties. Their lives and work justify the belief that they did much to promote the highest good of the people of this State, and as pioneers of civilization in this great Northwest contributed much to the wholesome influences that impart a respect for law and government.

CPSIA information can be obtained
at www.ICGtesting.com
Printed in the USA
LVHW061807240319
611664LV00010B/218/P

9 781375 847438